Cold Cases

Remarkable True Crime Mysteries That Remain Unsolved

Nolan Hawthorne

Cold Cases

Table of Contents

Chapter 1: The Enigma of Cold Cases

Understanding the Complexity of Unsolved Crimes

When diving into the world of unsolved crimes, one encounters a labyrinth of complexity that challenges both the mind and the heart. These mysteries, often shrouded in layers of ambiguity and speculation, demand a deeper understanding of the factors that contribute to their unresolved status. At the core, unsolved crimes are a tangle of incomplete narratives, each thread representing a missed opportunity, a lost piece of evidence, or a fleeting witness statement that remains just out of reach. To unravel these mysteries, one must first appreciate the intricate interplay of elements that transform a case from active investigation to cold.

A pivotal aspect of understanding unsolved crimes lies in the multifaceted nature of the evidence. Each crime scene is a puzzle, where every piece of evidence must be meticulously collected, cataloged, and analyzed. However, the passage of time can erode the quality and availability of this evidence. Physical traces such as DNA, fingerprints, and fibers are subject to degradation, while memories of witnesses fade, potentially leading to inconsistencies or complete loss of crucial testimonies. The initial investigation's thoroughness, or lack thereof, can significantly impact the trajectory of a case. A misstep in the early stages—be it a contaminated crime scene or an overlooked detail—can hinder the pursuit of justice for years or even decades.

The human element is another vital component in the complexity of unsolved crimes. Investigators, driven by a relentless pursuit of truth, often find themselves ensnared in a web of psychological and emotional challenges. The pressure to solve high-profile cases, coupled with the emotional toll of dealing with grieving families, can cloud judgment and affect decision-making. The burden of responsibility can weigh heavily on their shoulders, leading to burnout or a sense of defeat when leads dry up and the trail goes cold. This emotional terrain must be navigated with care and resilience, as the dedication of these individuals is often the only glimmer of hope for resolution.

The societal context in which a crime occurs also plays a crucial role in its unsolved status. Public interest can wax and wane, influenced by media coverage, social dynamics, and shifting cultural attitudes. In some cases, a lack of resources or prioritization within law enforcement agencies can result in cases being deprioritized or shelved indefinitely. Moreover, societal biases and prejudices may skew the focus of an investigation, leading to tunnel vision or the overlooking of potential suspects. Understanding these societal pressures is essential for comprehending why some crimes languish in the shadows, waiting for a break that may never come.

Technology, too, is a double-edged sword in the realm of unsolved crimes. While advances in forensic science offer new tools and methods for uncovering evidence, the rapid pace of technological change can render past techniques obsolete. Cold cases may lack the benefit of modern investigative methods, necessitating a reevaluation of evidence with fresh eyes and cutting-edge technologies. This evolution in forensic capabilities provides a glimmer of hope that cases once deemed unsolvable may yet be cracked, though it also highlights the challenges faced by investigators working with outdated methods.

The passage of time is both an adversary and an ally in the pursuit of solving unsolved crimes. While time can obscure the truth, it can also allow for new perspectives and insights to emerge. The persistence of investigators, journalists, and amateur sleuths can breathe new life into cold cases, driven by a shared desire for justice and closure. This perseverance, coupled with advancements in technology and evolving societal attitudes, fosters an environment where even the coldest cases can find resolution.

Psychologically, the allure of unsolved crimes captures the imagination of the public. The mystery and intrigue surrounding these cases invite endless speculation and theorizing, fueling a fascination that transcends time. This public interest can be both a boon and a burden, as media pressure can lead to rushed conclusions or sensationalized narratives that divert from the truth. The challenge lies in balancing public curiosity with the integrity of the investigation, ensuring that justice remains the primary focus.

The complexity of unsolved crimes is further compounded by the intersection of various fields of expertise. From forensic scientists and criminal profilers to legal experts and sociologists, a multidisciplinary approach is often necessary to untangle the intricate web of evidence and circumstance. Collaboration across these diverse domains can yield valuable insights, illuminating aspects of a case that may have previously gone unnoticed. This synergy of knowledge and skill is crucial in transforming a cold case into a solved one.

Ultimately, the complexity of unsolved crimes is a testament to the intricacies of human behavior and the unpredictability of life. Each case is a unique narrative, shaped by the actions and decisions of countless individuals. The challenge lies in piecing together these fragments to construct a coherent story that leads to truth and justice. It requires a delicate balance of perseverance, empathy, and innovation, qualities that define those who dedicate their lives to solving these enduring mysteries.

In grappling with the complexity of unsolved crimes, one gains a deeper appreciation for the dedication and tenacity required to bring resolution to these haunting cases. The pursuit of justice is a relentless journey, fraught with obstacles and setbacks, yet driven by an unwavering commitment to uncovering the truth. This commitment serves as a beacon of hope, guiding investigators, families, and society as a whole towards the possibility of closure and the restoration of peace.

The Factors That Lead to Cases Going Cold

A crime occurs. The initial flurry of activity sees detectives on the ground, forensic teams combing the area, witnesses interviewed, and every lead followed with vigor. Yet, as days turn into weeks and leads dry up, the momentum slows, and a once-active investigation begins to lose its heat. Several factors contribute to this frustrating transformation from a vibrant pursuit of justice to a stagnant, unsolved mystery.

One of the most significant contributors to cases going cold is the lack of immediate, useful evidence. In the early stages of an investigation, the availability and quality of evidence can make or break a case. Crime scenes are often chaotic, with potential evidence scattered across a wide area. If crucial evidence is missed, mishandled, or destroyed in those early moments, the chance of solving the case diminishes. Forensic technology, while advanced, relies heavily on the condition and quantity of the evidence collected. A single piece of overlooked DNA or a smudged fingerprint can mean the difference between identifying a suspect and reaching a dead end.

Witnesses play a pivotal role in the initial stages of any investigation. Their testimonies can provide vital clues and leads. However, human memory is notoriously unreliable, and the passage of time can distort or erase memories altogether. Witnesses may also be reluctant to come forward due to fear of retribution, mistrust of law enforcement, or a desire to avoid involvement in legal proceedings. In some cases, cultural or community dynamics may further discourage individuals from sharing what they know. As memories fade and witnesses become harder to track down, the likelihood of solving the case diminishes.

A case might also cool down due to insufficient resources. Law enforcement agencies often face budget constraints, understaffing, and a high volume of cases, stretching their resources thin. With limited personnel and funding, priority is given to cases with the best chance of resolution or those that attract significant media attention. As a result, less high-profile cases may receive less attention, leading to fewer dedicated resources and investigative efforts. The unfortunate reality is that many cases go cold simply because there aren't enough resources to keep them warm.

Jurisdictional challenges can further complicate investigations. Crimes that occur near jurisdictional boundaries or involve multiple agencies can lead to conflicts and miscommunication. Differences in procedures, priorities, and resources among agencies can hinder collaboration and information sharing, creating gaps in the investigation. In some instances, these jurisdictional challenges have allowed suspects to evade capture by exploiting the lack of coordination between agencies.

Public interest and media attention can greatly influence the trajectory of an investigation. High-profile cases often receive extensive coverage, which can generate leads and keep the investigation in the public eye. However, media sensationalism can also skew perceptions, ignite public pressure for quick resolutions, and lead to rushed or erroneous conclusions. Conversely, cases that receive little media attention may struggle to garner the necessary support and resources, causing them to fade into obscurity.

Technological limitations at the time a crime occurs can also contribute to cases going cold. While advancements in forensic science have revolutionized criminal investigations, older cases may not have benefited from these technologies. Evidence that was once deemed irrelevant or unusable might hold the key to solving the case with today's techniques. Unfortunately, without periodic re-evaluation of cold cases using modern methods, these technological gaps remain a barrier to resolution.

The passage of time affects every facet of an investigation. As the years go by, physical evidence degrades, witnesses become more difficult to locate, and memories fade. Suspects may relocate, change their identities, or even die, further complicating efforts to bring them to justice. Additionally, the original investigators may retire or be reassigned, resulting in a loss of institutional knowledge and continuity in the case. Each passing year adds another layer of difficulty, making it increasingly challenging to revive the case with fresh insights.

Cold cases also highlight the impact of societal and cultural factors on investigations. Changes in societal attitudes and cultural dynamics can influence the direction and focus of an investigation. For instance, crimes involving marginalized communities may not have received the same level of attention or urgency as those involving more privileged individuals. Historical biases and systemic inequalities can lead to the underreporting of crimes or the misallocation of resources, allowing certain cases to slip through the cracks.

Despite these challenges, hope endures for solving cold cases. Advances in technology, combined with the dedication of cold case units and the persistence of families and advocates, provide the potential for breakthroughs. Public interest can be reignited through media, documentaries, and true crime narratives, bringing fresh attention and resources to long-dormant cases. Collaborative efforts that transcend jurisdictional boundaries and utilize multidisciplinary approaches can also bridge gaps and uncover new leads.

Ultimately, understanding the factors that contribute to cases going cold is essential in addressing the systemic and procedural deficiencies that allow these mysteries to persist. By examining the interplay of evidence, witness dynamics, resources, jurisdictional challenges, public interest, technological limitations, and societal factors, we can better equip ourselves to prevent future cases from suffering a similar fate. The pursuit of justice in cold cases requires not only an unwavering commitment to the truth but also a concerted effort to learn from past mistakes and adapt to an ever-evolving investigative landscape.

The Role of Time in Obscuring Truth

Time, an ever-present force, shapes our perception and understanding of the world. In the realm of unsolved crimes, time can be both an ally and an adversary, influencing the trajectory of investigations and the eventual pursuit of truth. As hours turn into days, weeks, months, and even years, the passage of time complicates the task of uncovering the facts, allowing shadows to blur the lines between reality and speculation. Understanding how time obscures truth is crucial in unraveling the mysteries that cold cases present.

When a crime is first committed, the immediacy of the event provides investigators with a window of opportunity. Evidence is fresh, witnesses' memories are sharp, and the emotional impact of the crime is palpable. This initial period is critical for gathering and preserving evidence, as any delay can lead to contamination or degradation. Physical evidence—such as blood, fibers, or fingerprints—can be compromised by environmental factors or human error, losing its reliability over time. As days go by, the condition of this evidence deteriorates, diminishing its value and complicating efforts to connect it to potential suspects.

Witness testimony, often considered one of the most valuable tools in an investigation, is particularly vulnerable to the ravages of time. The human brain, while remarkable, is prone to misremembering or altering details. Memories can fade, merge, or even be replaced by false recollections, especially when influenced by external factors like media coverage or conversations with others. The longer the time between the event and a witness's testimony, the greater the likelihood of inaccuracies. This erosion of memory can lead to conflicting accounts and unreliable narratives, obscuring the truth and hindering the investigative process.

Time also impacts the availability and willingness of witnesses. As years pass, people move away, change contact information, or pass on, making them difficult to locate. Those who were once eager to help may become less inclined to engage with law enforcement due to fear, mistrust, or a desire to leave the past behind. This attrition of witnesses reduces the pool of firsthand information, leaving investigators to rely on secondhand accounts or incomplete records.

The emotional landscape of those involved in a case—families, investigators, and communities—evolves over time. For families of victims, the passage of time can be both a source of agony and a catalyst for healing. The initial shock and grief may give way to a quieter, more enduring pain, characterized by unanswered questions and unfulfilled justice. This emotional toll can influence their interactions with law enforcement and media, affecting the dissemination of information. Conversely, the passage of time can allow for personal growth and resilience, motivating families to advocate for renewed attention and resources for their loved one's case.

For investigators, the relentless march of time can lead to frustration and disillusionment. The pressure to solve a case is immense, and as time wears on, the weight of unresolved cases accumulates. Investigators may face burnout or be reassigned to more pressing matters, resulting in a loss of continuity and institutional knowledge. This turnover can leave gaps in the investigation, as new detectives may not have the same insights or connections as their predecessors. Despite these challenges, the dedication of investigators often remains unwavering, driven by a commitment to uncovering the truth for victims and their families.

Communities, too, are affected by the passage of time. Public interest in a case may wane as new events capture the spotlight. This shift in attention can lead to a decrease in resources and support for ongoing investigations, further complicating efforts to keep the case alive. However, time can also foster a sense of collective memory and identity, with communities rallying to keep the story of an unsolved crime in the public consciousness. This enduring interest can reignite media coverage and attract fresh eyes to the case, offering new perspectives and potential breakthroughs.

The role of time in obscuring truth is not solely a hindrance; it can also provide opportunities for solving cold cases. Advances in technology and forensic science continue to evolve, offering new tools and methods for analyzing evidence. Cold cases benefit from these innovations, as previously overlooked or unusable evidence can be reexamined with modern techniques. DNA analysis, for instance, has revolutionized the ability to identify suspects and exonerate the innocent, even decades after a crime was committed. The passage of time allows for these breakthroughs to occur, breathing new life into cases once deemed unsolvable.

Furthermore, time can bring about changes in societal attitudes and legal frameworks, prompting a reevaluation of past cases. Shifts in cultural norms and values may lead to increased attention and resources for crimes involving marginalized communities that were previously neglected. Legal reforms and changes in law enforcement practices can also improve the handling and prioritization of cold cases, creating an environment more conducive to uncovering the truth.

The intersection of time and truth in unsolved crimes is a complex and multifaceted dynamic. While time can obscure and complicate the pursuit of justice, it also holds the potential for resolution through technological advancements, renewed interest, and societal change. Recognizing the dual nature of time's impact on investigations is essential for those seeking to navigate the challenges and opportunities it presents.

In the end, the role of time in obscuring truth is a reminder of the persistence and resilience required to solve cold cases. It underscores the importance of maintaining hope and dedication, even when faced with the passage of years. Time, while often seen as an adversary, can ultimately become an ally in the quest for justice, revealing the truth one step at a time.

Psychological Impact on Investigators and Families

Time, an ever-present force, shapes our perception and understanding of the world. In the realm of unsolved crimes, time can be both an ally and an adversary, influencing the trajectory of investigations and the eventual pursuit of truth. As hours turn into days, weeks, months, and even years, the passage of time complicates the task of uncovering the facts, allowing shadows to blur the lines between reality and speculation. Understanding how time obscures truth is crucial in unraveling the mysteries that cold cases present.

When a crime is first committed, the immediacy of the event provides investigators with a window of opportunity. Evidence is fresh, witnesses' memories are sharp, and the emotional impact of the crime is palpable. This initial period is critical for gathering and preserving evidence, as any delay can lead to contamination or degradation. Physical evidence—such as blood, fibers, or fingerprints—can be compromised by environmental factors or human error, losing its reliability over time. As days go by, the condition of this evidence deteriorates, diminishing its value and complicating efforts to connect it to potential suspects.

Witness testimony, often considered one of the most valuable tools in an investigation, is particularly vulnerable to the ravages of time. The human brain, while remarkable, is prone to misremembering or altering details. Memories can fade, merge, or even be replaced by false recollections, especially when influenced by external factors like media coverage or conversations with others. The longer the time between the event and a witness's testimony, the greater the likelihood of inaccuracies. This erosion of memory can lead to conflicting accounts and unreliable narratives, obscuring the truth and hindering the investigative process.

Time also impacts the availability and willingness of witnesses. As years pass, people move away, change contact information, or pass on, making them difficult to locate. Those who were once eager to help may become less inclined to engage with law enforcement due to fear, mistrust, or a desire to leave the past behind. This attrition of witnesses reduces the pool of firsthand information, leaving investigators to rely on secondhand accounts or incomplete records.

The emotional landscape of those involved in a case—families, investigators, and communities—evolves over time. For families of victims, the passage of time can be both a source of agony and a catalyst for healing. The initial shock and grief may give way to a quieter, more enduring pain, characterized by unanswered questions and unfulfilled justice. This emotional toll can influence their interactions with law enforcement and media, affecting the dissemination of information. Conversely, the passage of time can allow for personal growth and resilience, motivating families to advocate for renewed attention and resources for their loved one's case.

For investigators, the relentless march of time can lead to frustration and disillusionment. The pressure to solve a case is immense, and as time wears on, the weight of unresolved cases accumulates. Investigators may face burnout or be reassigned to more pressing matters, resulting in a loss of continuity and institutional knowledge. This turnover can leave gaps in the investigation, as new detectives may not have the same insights or connections as their predecessors. Despite these challenges, the dedication of investigators often remains unwavering, driven by a commitment to uncovering the truth for victims and their families.

Communities, too, are affected by the passage of time. Public interest in a case may wane as new events capture the spotlight. This shift in attention can lead to a decrease in resources and support for ongoing investigations, further complicating efforts to keep the case alive. However, time can also foster a sense of collective memory and identity, with communities rallying to keep the story of an unsolved crime in the public consciousness. This enduring interest can reignite media coverage and attract fresh eyes to the case, offering new perspectives and potential breakthroughs.

The role of time in obscuring truth is not solely a hindrance; it can also provide opportunities for solving cold cases. Advances in technology and forensic science continue to evolve, offering new tools and methods for analyzing evidence. Cold cases benefit from these innovations, as previously overlooked or unusable evidence can be reexamined with modern techniques. DNA analysis, for instance, has revolutionized the ability to identify suspects and exonerate the innocent, even decades after a crime was committed. The passage of time allows for these breakthroughs to occur, breathing new life into cases once deemed unsolvable.

Furthermore, time can bring about changes in societal attitudes and legal frameworks, prompting a reevaluation of past cases. Shifts in cultural norms and values may lead to increased attention and resources for crimes involving marginalized communities that were previously neglected. Legal reforms and changes in law enforcement practices can also improve the handling and prioritization of cold cases, creating an environment more conducive to uncovering the truth.

The intersection of time and truth in unsolved crimes is a complex and multifaceted dynamic. While time can obscure and complicate the pursuit of justice, it also holds the potential for resolution through technological advancements, renewed interest, and societal change. Recognizing the dual nature of time's impact on investigations is essential for those seeking to navigate the challenges and opportunities it presents.

In the end, the role of time in obscuring truth is a reminder of the persistence and resilience required to solve cold cases. It underscores the importance of maintaining hope and dedication, even when faced with the passage of years. Time, while often seen as an adversary, can ultimately become an ally in the quest for justice, revealing the truth one step at a time.

The Fascination with the Unsolved

Mysteries have always captivated the human mind, and unsolved crimes stand as some of the most intriguing puzzles of our time. The allure of the unsolved lies in its ability to tantalize, challenge, and provoke the imagination. It's a dance between reality and the unknown, where every unturned stone and unanswered question beckons the curious to delve deeper. This fascination is not just a modern phenomenon; it is woven into the fabric of human history, from ancient tales of lost civilizations to the cryptic narratives of unsolved disappearances and enigmatic murders.

The human psyche is inherently drawn to mystery. There is a primal urge to seek answers, to bring order to chaos, and to find meaning in the inexplicable. Unsolved crimes tap into this deep-seated instinct, presenting a challenge that is both intellectual and emotional. The absence of resolution leaves a void that compels us to fill it with theories, speculation, and conjecture. We become detectives in our own right, piecing together available information, constructing narratives, and exploring the possibilities that lie hidden within the shadows of uncertainty.

One of the most compelling aspects of unsolved crimes is the freedom they offer for interpretation. Unlike resolved cases, where the narrative is complete and the facts are established, unsolved cases remain open-ended, inviting endless exploration and debate. This openness allows individuals to engage with the mystery on a personal level, projecting their own experiences, biases, and beliefs onto the case. It becomes a canvas for the imagination, where the lines between fact and fiction blur, and the story becomes as much about the investigator as it is about the crime itself.

The media plays a significant role in shaping our fascination with unsolved crimes. From the earliest days of print journalism to today's digital age, media coverage has brought these mysteries into the public consciousness, often sensationalizing them to capture attention and spark intrigue. Documentaries, podcasts, and true crime shows have further fueled this interest, offering in-depth analyses and dramatizations that immerse audiences in the complexities of each case. This cultural phenomenon not only keeps unsolved crimes in the spotlight but also fosters a community of amateur sleuths and enthusiasts who dedicate their time and energy to uncovering new leads and insights.

The appeal of unsolved crimes is also rooted in their inherent drama and tension. They are real-life whodunits, complete with twists, turns, and cliffhangers that rival the most gripping works of fiction. Each unsolved case is a narrative waiting to be completed, a story with missing chapters that invite us to imagine what might have been. The stakes are high, involving real people with real emotions, and the consequences of each revelation carry weight and significance. This blend of reality and storytelling creates an immersive experience that captivates and engages, drawing us into a world where the boundaries of truth and speculation are constantly shifting.

The psychological dimension of unsolved crimes adds another layer to their fascination. These cases often involve complex personalities and motives, presenting a window into the darker aspects of human nature. The enigmatic figures at the center of these mysteries—be they victims, suspects, or investigators—become characters in a larger narrative, each with their own secrets, desires, and vulnerabilities. This exploration of the human condition resonates with our innate curiosity about the motivations and behaviors that drive people to commit or become entangled in such acts.

Unsolved crimes also provide an opportunity for individuals to engage with the concept of justice. The lack of resolution in these cases highlights the imperfections of the legal and investigative systems, prompting reflection on the nature of justice and its limitations. For some, this is a call to action, inspiring advocacy for cold case investigations, legal reforms, and the pursuit of truth. For others, it is a reminder of the fragility of justice and the need for vigilance in ensuring that every effort is made to solve these lingering mysteries.

The enduring fascination with unsolved crimes is a testament to their power to captivate, challenge, and inspire. They are a mirror reflecting our deepest fears, hopes, and curiosities, offering a unique lens through which to explore the complexities of human nature and society. As long as there are mysteries left unsolved, the allure of the unknown will continue to beckon, inviting us to embark on a journey of discovery and wonder.

The cultural impact of unsolved crimes extends beyond mere entertainment or intellectual curiosity. They serve as a touchstone for collective memory, preserving the stories of those who have been lost to time and circumstance. In keeping these cases alive in the public's mind, we honor the individuals at the heart of these mysteries, ensuring that their stories are not forgotten and that the quest for answers continues. This sense of connection and remembrance is a powerful motivator, driving individuals and communities to seek closure and justice for those who can no longer speak for themselves.

Unsolved crimes also challenge us to confront our own limitations and biases. They remind us that truth is often elusive, shaped by incomplete information and subjective interpretation. In grappling with these uncertainties, we are forced to consider the complexity of human nature and the myriad factors that contribute to the unfolding of events. This introspection fosters empathy and understanding, encouraging us to approach each mystery with an open mind and a willingness to question our assumptions.

The allure of unsolved crimes is a multifaceted phenomenon, encompassing elements of intrigue, drama, psychology, justice, and human connection. It is a reflection of our deepest instincts and desires, a testament to our unyielding quest for knowledge and understanding. As we continue to explore these mysteries, we are reminded of the power of storytelling and the enduring impact of the unresolved. The journey may be fraught with challenges and uncertainties, but it is one that enriches our understanding of ourselves and the world around us.

Chapter 2: Notorious Cold Cases from Around the World

The Disappearance of Amelia Earhart: Aviation's Greatest Mystery

Amelia Earhart's name conjures images of daring flights and groundbreaking achievements, but it is her mysterious disappearance that has immortalized her in the annals of history. The story of her vanishing is one of aviation's most captivating enigmas, a puzzle that has intrigued experts and enthusiasts alike for decades. On July 2, 1937, Earhart and her navigator, Fred Noonan, embarked on the final leg of their ambitious attempt to circumnavigate the globe, only to disappear without a trace over the vast expanse of the Pacific Ocean. The circumstances surrounding their disappearance have sparked numerous theories and investigations, yet the truth remains elusive.

The journey began with high hopes and meticulous planning. Earhart, already a celebrated aviator, aimed to be the first woman to fly around the world. Her chosen route was an ambitious one, spanning approximately 29,000 miles. By the time they reached Lae, New Guinea, they had successfully covered over 22,000 miles. The next destination was Howland Island, a remote speck in the Pacific, which posed significant navigational challenges. The island's diminutive size and the expanse of ocean surrounding it required precise coordination between Earhart's aircraft and the ground support team waiting with radio guidance and fuel.

As Earhart and Noonan took off from Lae, the world watched with anticipation. Communication was key to their success, yet it was fraught with difficulties. The Electra, Earhart's aircraft, was equipped with a radio, but technical issues plagued their transmissions. Despite these problems, they maintained contact with the Itasca, a U.S. Coast Guard cutter stationed near Howland Island, which served as their primary point of contact. However, the communication was sporadic and fraught with misunderstandings, leaving the crew of the Itasca increasingly anxious as the hours passed.

The last confirmed transmission from Earhart indicated they were flying on a line of position, a navigational method used when the exact location is uncertain. She reported being low on fuel and unable to locate Howland Island. Then, silence ensued. Despite extensive search efforts by the U.S. Navy and Coast Guard, no trace of the Electra, Earhart, or Noonan was found. The official search was called off after two weeks, leaving behind a mystery that would continue to captivate the world.

Over the years, numerous theories have emerged, each attempting to explain the fate of Amelia Earhart and Fred Noonan. One of the most prominent theories suggests that they ran out of fuel and crashed into the Pacific Ocean, their aircraft sinking to the depths, never to be seen again. This theory is supported by the lack of any physical evidence on nearby islands and the vastness of the ocean, which would have made recovery efforts extraordinarily difficult.

Another theory posits that Earhart and Noonan may have landed on an uninhabited island, such as Gardner Island (now

Nikumaroro), part of modern-day Kiribati. Proponents of this theory point to anecdotal evidence from island inhabitants and the discovery of artifacts that could potentially be linked to Earhart. Despite several expeditions to the island, no conclusive evidence has been found to confirm this hypothesis.

A more controversial theory suggests that Earhart and Noonan were captured by Japanese forces, suspecting them of espionage. This theory, while less widely accepted, is fueled by reports and anecdotes from the time, although no credible evidence has been presented to substantiate these claims. The lack of documentation and the secretive nature of wartime operations have left this theory largely in the realm of speculation.

The fascination with Amelia Earhart's disappearance extends beyond the mystery itself. Earhart was a trailblazer, a woman who defied societal norms and pushed the boundaries of aviation. Her story resonates with themes of adventure, courage, and the pursuit of dreams, making her disappearance not just a historical mystery but a narrative of human ambition and resilience. The lack of closure adds an element of poignancy to her legacy, reminding us of the risks inherent in the quest for exploration and discovery.

The search for answers continues to this day, with modern technology offering new avenues for investigation. Advances in sonar and underwater exploration have renewed efforts to locate the wreckage of the Electra, while archival research and forensic analysis have provided fresh insights into the events leading up to the disappearance. Each new piece of information adds to the tapestry of the mystery, keeping the story of Amelia Earhart alive in the public's imagination.

The legacy of Amelia Earhart is one of inspiration and intrigue. Her disappearance remains one of the greatest mysteries of the 20th century, a testament to the enduring allure of the unknown. As we reflect on her life and achievements, we are reminded of the spirit of exploration that drives humanity to seek out new frontiers, even in the face of uncertainty. The mystery of her fate serves as a poignant reminder that, despite our best efforts, some questions may never be fully answered, leaving us to ponder the possibilities and continue the search for truth.

The Hinterkaifeck Murders: A Farmhouse Shrouded in Mystery

Nestled in the Bavarian countryside, the Hinterkaifeck farm stood isolated, a simple homestead surrounded by fields and forests. In 1922, this seemingly serene setting became the stage for one of Germany's most enigmatic and gruesome unsolved crimes. The Hinterkaifeck murders captured the attention of a nation and have since become a haunting tale of intrigue and horror that continues to perplex investigators and enthusiasts alike.

The events unfolded in late March, when Andreas Gruber, the head of the family, noticed strange occurrences around the farm. Footprints leading from the woods ended at the farmhouse, yet no tracks led back. The sounds of footsteps echoed in the attic, and keys disappeared, only to reappear inexplicably. Despite these unsettling signs, the Gruber family continued with their daily lives, unaware of the impending tragedy.

On the evening of March 31st, 1922, a chilling silence descended upon Hinterkaifeck. Over the course of the night, six members of the Gruber family were brutally murdered: Andreas, his wife Cäzilia, their widowed daughter Viktoria, her two children, Cäzilia and Josef, and the family's maid, Maria Baumgartner, who had begun working there just hours before the massacre. The victims were lured one by one to the barn where they were bludgeoned to death with a mattock. The killer then moved inside the farmhouse to finish the grim task.

The discovery of the murders came days later when neighbors, concerned about the family's absence from Sunday church service and school, decided to investigate. What they found was a scene of unimaginable horror. The bodies had been carefully concealed beneath hay in the barn, while those inside the house were discovered in their beds. The animals on the farm had been tended to, and smoke had been seen rising from the chimney in the days following the murders, suggesting the perpetrator remained at the scene, going about daily routines as if nothing had happened.

The investigation that followed was extensive yet fraught with challenges and peculiarities. Early police work was hampered by curious onlookers who trampled the crime scene, inadvertently destroying potential evidence. Despite the best efforts of law enforcement, the case remained unsolved, with no decisive leads pointing to a suspect. Theories and speculation proliferated, each more puzzling than the last.

One of the prevailing theories centered on a family member as the possible perpetrator. The Grubers were known to have dark secrets, including allegations of an incestuous relationship between Andreas and Viktoria. This theory suggested that deep-seated familial tensions may have erupted into violence, though no concrete evidence supported this notion. Another theory pointed to a disgruntled local or former worker with a vendetta against the family. Yet, despite thorough questioning of those connected to the farm, none emerged as a viable suspect.

A more sinister possibility involved a stranger or vagrant passing through the area. The isolated location of Hinterkaifeck made it an easy target for an outsider seeking shelter or sustenance. However, this theory failed to explain the intimate knowledge the murderer seemed to possess about the farm and its routines, as well as the apparent comfort with which they remained on the property after the crime.

The Hinterkaifeck murders also inspired supernatural explanations, with some speculating that the farm was cursed or haunted. These theories, though intriguing, offered little in the way of practical solutions, serving only to deepen the mystery surrounding the case.

Despite numerous attempts to solve the murders over the years, including modern forensic analysis and psychological profiling, the case remains as elusive as ever. The passage of time has only added to its mystique, with each new generation of investigators and amateur sleuths drawn to the challenge of unraveling the enigma of Hinterkaifeck.

The legacy of the Hinterkaifeck murders extends beyond the macabre details of the crime itself. It is a story that speaks to the human fascination with the unknown and the darkness that can lurk within the familiar. The case remains a testament to the complexities of human nature and the enduring power of mystery to captivate and confound.

The Hinterkaifeck farmhouse, long since demolished, lives on in the collective memory as a symbol of unresolved tragedy. The unanswered questions and chilling details continue to fuel speculation and debate, ensuring that the story of Hinterkaifeck remains an indelible part of both local folklore and the broader tapestry of unsolved crimes.

For those captivated by the mystery, the Hinterkaifeck murders serve as a reminder of the enduring allure of the unknown. The case challenges us to confront the limits of our understanding and the depths of our curiosity, inviting us to explore the shadows of history in search of truth.

The Beaumont Children: Vanished Without a Trace

A hot summer's day on January 26, 1966, in Glenelg, a bustling suburb of Adelaide, Australia, marked the beginning of one of the most infamous unsolved cases in Australian history—the disappearance of the Beaumont children. Jane, Arnna, and Grant Beaumont, aged nine, seven, and four respectively, set off for a day at the beach, a familiar and routine outing that belied the darkness that would soon envelop their family and community. This seemingly ordinary day would become etched in the collective memory, as the children vanished without a trace, leaving behind a mystery that has haunted the nation for decades.

The Beaumont children were well-acquainted with the short bus ride to Glenelg Beach, a destination they had visited numerous times before. Their mother, Nancy Beaumont, waved them off that morning, expecting them to return by midday, as they had promised. When the afternoon wore on with no sign of the children, concern turned to panic. By evening, the Beaumonts' quiet home was filled with worry, and the police were notified. The community was thrust into a state of shock as search efforts began, with the hope of finding the children safe and sound.

Despite an immediate and extensive investigation, the case presented few concrete leads. Witnesses reported seeing the children at the beach in the company of a tall, blond man, estimated to be in his mid-thirties. This man was described as friendly and engaging, playing with the children before leaving the area together. The details of this encounter provided the police with a potential suspect, yet the identity of this man remained elusive. Despite eyewitness accounts and composite sketches, he was never identified, and the trail quickly grew cold.

The disappearance of the Beaumont children captured the public's imagination, becoming a focal point for media coverage and public discourse. The case was unprecedented in its scope and impact, with the police receiving thousands of calls and alleged sightings from across the country and even internationally. The investigation spanned decades, encompassing numerous leads, suspects, and theories, yet none yielded definitive answers.

One of the most persistent theories involved a possible connection to known pedophiles operating in the area at the time. Some investigators speculated that the children's disappearance was linked to an organized network of offenders, a hypothesis that, while plausible, lacked tangible evidence. The inability to substantiate this theory left it largely in the realm of speculation, further compounding the mystery.

Another avenue explored was the possibility that the children had been abducted by someone close to the family or an acquaintance. This theory was fueled by the apparent ease with which the children interacted with the unknown man at the beach, suggesting a level of familiarity and trust. However, extensive investigation into the family's acquaintances and social circle revealed no viable suspects, leaving this theory without resolution.

The case took an unexpected turn in the 1970s when a convicted child sex offender, Bevan Spencer von Einem, emerged as a person of interest. Known for his involvement in the infamous "Family Murders" in Adelaide, von Einem was speculated to have ties to the Beaumont case. Despite his heinous crimes and the circumstantial connections to the Beaumont children, no concrete evidence linked him to their disappearance, and he was never charged in relation to the case.

The Beaumont children's disappearance was not only a personal tragedy for their family but also a catalyst for societal change in Australia. It prompted a reevaluation of parenting norms and attitudes toward child safety, shifting the cultural landscape in ways that would resonate for generations. The case underscored the need for heightened awareness and vigilance, leading to reforms in law enforcement practices and community engagement in the protection of children.

Despite the passage of time, the Beaumont case remains active in the minds of investigators and the public alike. Advances in forensic technology and investigative techniques offer hope that new leads or evidence may one day emerge, shedding light on the fate of the Beaumont children. The enduring mystery continues to inspire amateur sleuths, journalists, and researchers who remain committed to uncovering the truth.

The disappearance of the Beaumont children is a poignant reminder of the fragility of innocence and the enduring impact of unanswered questions. It serves as a testament to the resilience of a community united in the face of tragedy, and the unwavering determination to seek justice and closure. As the years pass, the case remains a haunting chapter in the annals of unsolved mysteries, a story of loss and longing that continues to echo in the hearts of those who remember the smiling faces of Jane, Arnna, and Grant Beaumont.

For those who continue to search for answers, the Beaumont case is a symbol of hope and perseverance. It challenges us to confront the complexities of human nature and the shadows that can lie hidden beneath the surface of everyday life. The quest for resolution is a journey that transcends time, driven by the desire to honor the memory of the Beaumont children and bring peace to their family.

The Case of the Somerton Man: A Puzzle from the Past

On December 1, 1948, the quiet seaside town of Somerton in Adelaide, Australia, became the epicenter of one of the most puzzling mysteries of the 20th century. A man's lifeless body was discovered propped against the seawall at Somerton Beach. Dressed impeccably in a suit and polished shoes, the man presented a curious enigma. He carried no identification, and the tags had been meticulously removed from his clothing, leaving behind a riddle that has defied resolution for over seven decades.

The initial investigation into the man's identity and cause of death set the stage for an intricate puzzle. Despite extensive efforts, no one came forward to identify the body. The absence of identification documents and the removal of clothing labels suggested a calculated attempt to obscure the man's identity. His physical appearance, well-groomed and healthy, offered no clues to his origins or purpose for being in Somerton. The autopsy revealed an inconclusive cause of death, with the possibility of poisoning considered but unproven, adding another layer of intrigue to the unfolding mystery.

A small, tightly rolled piece of paper found in a hidden pocket of the man's trousers provided the first of many cryptic clues. Bearing the words "Tamam Shud," meaning "ended" or "finished" in Persian, the scrap appeared to have been torn from a rare edition of "The Rubaiyat of Omar Khayyam," an enigmatic collection of poems. This discovery would lead investigators down a labyrinthine path, connecting the case to a network of intrigue, espionage, and unconfirmed associations with global events of the time.

The search for the source of the torn page led to another breakthrough. A copy of the book, with a missing final page, was found in an abandoned car near the site of the discovery. Inside the book, investigators found a perplexing sequence of letters that appeared to be a code. Despite numerous attempts by cryptographers and amateur codebreakers, the meaning of the sequence remains undeciphered, leaving speculation about its significance and whether it holds the key to understanding the man's identity and demise.

The case took an unexpected turn with the discovery of a suitcase at Adelaide's main railway station, believed to belong to the mysterious man. Inside, investigators found clothing consistent with the man's size and style, again with identifying labels removed. Among the items were tools suggesting an association with engineering or technical work, further complicating efforts to construct a coherent narrative of the man's life and purpose.

A significant yet puzzling connection emerged when a nurse, identified only as "Jestyn," was linked to the case. She lived near Somerton Beach and reportedly owned a copy of "The Rubaiyat of Omar Khayyam," which she had given to an acquaintance. Despite this intriguing link, Jestyn denied any knowledge of the man, and her involvement, if any, remains speculative. This connection fueled theories ranging from romantic entanglement to espionage, yet no definitive evidence has confirmed her role in the mystery.

The possibility of espionage has been a persistent theory throughout the investigation, given the post-World War II context and the man's potential technical background. Some have speculated that he was a spy or an operative involved in clandestine activities, possibly connected to the geopolitical tensions of the era. However, this theory, while compelling, remains conjectural, with no concrete evidence to substantiate such claims.

Decades after the discovery, the intrigue surrounding the case has only intensified, with numerous attempts to solve the mystery through modern forensic techniques and genetic analysis. In recent years, exhumation of the body and advanced DNA testing have been proposed as potential methods to finally uncover the man's identity and origins. These efforts reflect the enduring fascination with the case and the desire to bring closure to one of history's most elusive puzzles.

The Somerton Man case is a testament to the complexity of human identity and the allure of the unknown. It challenges us to confront the limitations of our understanding and the depths of our curiosity. The mystery transcends time, capturing the imagination of each new generation of investigators, historians, and amateur sleuths drawn to the enigma of the unknown man on Somerton Beach.

This case also highlights the intricate interplay between evidence, interpretation, and the human desire for resolution. Each clue, from the torn page to the coded message, invites us to explore the boundaries of logic and intuition, encouraging us to consider the myriad possibilities that lie hidden within the shadows of history.

For those captivated by the Somerton Man, the search for answers is a journey of discovery and introspection. It is a reminder of the enduring power of mystery to inspire and challenge, urging us to look beyond the surface and delve into the complexities of the human experience. As we continue to seek understanding, the case remains an indelible part of our collective consciousness, a puzzle that beckons us to unravel its secrets and honor the memory of the unknown man who walked into the pages of history.

Insights from Other Global Cold Cases

Cold cases hold a unique place in the realm of criminal investigations, representing mysteries that have resisted resolution despite the passage of time. These cases, drawn from diverse corners of the globe, share common threads of intrigue, complexity, and the relentless pursuit of truth. By examining insights from notable cold cases worldwide, we can glean valuable lessons about the challenges and opportunities in solving long-standing mysteries.

The case of the Zodiac Killer in the United States serves as a prime example of a cold case that continues to captivate investigators and the public alike. Operating in the late 1960s and early 1970s, the Zodiac Killer is linked to a series of brutal murders in Northern California. The killer taunted police and media with cryptic letters and ciphers, some of which remain unsolved to this day. Despite extensive investigations, the identity of the Zodiac Killer remains unknown. This case highlights the importance of innovative forensic techniques, as modern DNA analysis and digital technology offer new hope in deciphering the killer's identity. It underscores the potential for advancements in science to unlock secrets that have long eluded traditional investigative methods.

Another intriguing cold case is the disappearance of British child Madeleine McCann, who vanished from a holiday resort in Portugal in 2007. The case attracted international attention and sparked a massive search effort. Despite numerous leads and extensive media coverage, Madeleine's whereabouts remain unknown. This case illustrates the challenges of international cooperation in criminal investigations. It emphasizes the need for effective collaboration between law enforcement agencies across borders, as well as the role of public awareness and media in keeping cases alive in the public consciousness.

In Japan, the mysterious murder of the Setagaya family in 2000 stands as a chilling reminder of the complexity of cold cases. The Miyazawa family was brutally killed in their Tokyo home, with the perpetrator leaving behind a wealth of physical evidence, including fingerprints and clothing. Despite this, the case remains unsolved, baffling investigators and criminologists. This case highlights the limitations of evidence when not matched to a suspect within existing databases. It also demonstrates the importance of meticulous crime scene management and the potential for overlooked details to hold the key to solving a case.

The case of Swedish Prime Minister Olof Palme, who was assassinated in 1986, provides another perspective on cold cases. Palme was shot dead on a Stockholm street, and despite numerous suspects and extensive investigations, the case remained unsolved for decades. In 2020, Swedish authorities identified a suspect they believe was responsible, though the individual had died years earlier. This case underscores the potential for breakthroughs even after significant time has elapsed. It also highlights the role of public and political pressure in driving investigations forward, as well as the need for dedicated resources and perseverance in pursuing justice.

South Africa's "Graveyard Rapist" case is another example of a cold case that saw resolution through persistence and technological advancements. The perpetrator was linked to numerous sexual assaults and murders in the 1990s. Advances in DNA technology eventually led to his identification and conviction years later. This case exemplifies the power of forensic science in providing closure to victims and their families, showcasing the importance of preserving evidence for future analysis as technology evolves.

The disappearance of Malaysia Airlines Flight MH370 in 2014 remains one of the most perplexing aviation mysteries in recent history. The aircraft vanished over the Indian Ocean with 239 people on board, and despite extensive search efforts, the wreckage has never been conclusively located. This case highlights the challenges of investigating incidents involving complex systems and vast geographical areas. It emphasizes the need for international cooperation, transparency, and the use of cutting-edge technology in search and rescue operations. The ongoing search for answers serves as a reminder of the resilience and determination required in the face of uncertainty.

Insights from these global cold cases reveal several common themes and lessons. The advancement of forensic science and technology plays a crucial role in solving cases that have long resisted resolution. The preservation and re-examination of evidence, coupled with the development of new techniques, can yield breakthroughs even decades after the fact. Additionally, effective collaboration between law enforcement agencies, both domestically and internationally, is essential in addressing the complexities of modern investigations.

Public engagement and media coverage can also influence the trajectory of cold cases. Keeping a case in the public eye can generate new leads, maintain pressure on authorities, and ensure that victims and their families are not forgotten. However, it is important to balance public interest with the integrity of the investigation, ensuring that misinformation or sensationalism does not hinder progress.

The perseverance and dedication of investigators, both professional and amateur, are vital in the pursuit of justice. Cold cases demand a relentless commitment to uncovering the truth, often requiring a fresh perspective or innovative approach to overcome obstacles. The stories of those who continue to seek answers serve as a testament to the enduring human spirit and the unyielding quest for justice.

Ultimately, each cold case is a narrative waiting to be completed, a puzzle with pieces scattered across time and space. By studying these cases, we gain insights not only into the nature of crime and investigation but also into the broader human experience. The lessons learned from these mysteries remind us of the complexities of the world we live in and the enduring hope that, one day, the truth will emerge from the shadows.

Chapter 3: Unsolved Mysteries That Captured the Public Imagination

The Zodiac Killer: A Cipher of Fear

In the shadowy corners of Northern California, a figure emerged in the late 1960s whose identity and motives remain one of the most fearsome enigmas in criminal history. The Zodiac Killer, as he came to be known, was responsible for a series of brutal murders and a chilling campaign of taunts directed at law enforcement and the public. This case, marked by cryptic letters and unsolved ciphers, has fascinated and frustrated generations of investigators, leaving a legacy of fear and intrigue that still lingers today.

The Zodiac's reign of terror began in December 1968 with the murder of two teenagers, Betty Lou Jensen and David Faraday, on a quiet road in Vallejo, California. They were the first known victims in a spree that would claim at least five confirmed lives. The killer's modus operandi varied, but his hallmark was his bold communication with the press and police, relishing the chaos and fear he spread. In July 1969, another attack left Darlene Ferrin dead and Michael Mageau severely injured, providing the first witness account of the elusive assailant.

What set the Zodiac Killer apart from other criminals was his penchant for puzzles. He sent a series of letters to local newspapers, each containing a cipher or riddle that he claimed would reveal his identity. The most notorious of these was the

408-symbol cipher, which he demanded be published or he would kill again. The cryptogram was eventually cracked by a schoolteacher and his wife, revealing a message that boasted of his love for killing and the thrill of hunting humans. Yet, crucially, it did not disclose his name, maintaining the shroud of anonymity he so carefully orchestrated.

The Zodiac's communication was not limited to ciphers. He sent numerous letters detailing his crimes, threatening more violence, and taunting the police for their inability to catch him. His letters often included peculiar symbols and a crosshair-like logo that became synonymous with his identity. In one particularly chilling letter, he claimed to have attached a flashlight to his gun for accuracy, showcasing a calculated and methodical approach to his crimes.

Despite the taunting, the Zodiac Killer's identity eluded law enforcement. Descriptions from surviving victims and witnesses varied, complicating efforts to create an accurate profile. The killer was described as a white male, possibly in his late twenties or early thirties, but beyond that, details were scarce. The investigation was hampered by the lack of forensic technology available at the time, leaving detectives reliant on physical evidence and eyewitness testimony that often led to dead ends.

The Zodiac's most infamous attack occurred on September 27, 1969, when Bryan Hartnell and Cecelia Shepard were brutally stabbed at Lake Berryessa. The killer, in an unusual move, approached the couple wearing an executioner's hood and a bib-like garment emblazoned with his crosshair symbol. After the attack, he left a message on their car door, providing details of the crime and his signature symbol. Cecelia Shepard succumbed to her injuries, but Bryan Hartnell survived and provided crucial details about the encounter, though they failed to lead to an arrest.

The final confirmed murder attributed to the Zodiac occurred in San Francisco on October 11, 1969, when cab driver Paul Stine was shot in the city's Presidio Heights neighborhood. This marked a departure from the killer's previous methods, as it involved a single victim and took place in an urban environment. The Zodiac sent a piece of Stine's bloodied shirt to the San Francisco Chronicle, further cementing his flair for the macabre. Despite a swift police response and numerous tips, the killer once again slipped away, leaving only a trail of fear and confusion.

Over time, the Zodiac's communications dwindled, but his influence endured. The case inspired widespread speculation and numerous theories regarding his identity. Amateur sleuths and professional investigators have proposed various suspects, yet none have been definitively linked to all the crimes. Theories have ranged from plausible to far-fetched, encompassing individuals with potential connections to the Bay Area and those with a penchant for cryptography or military backgrounds.

The Zodiac's use of ciphers has been a focal point of the investigation. While some have been solved, others, like the 340-character cipher sent in November 1969, remained a mystery for over 50 years until it was finally deciphered in 2020. This solution did not provide the long-sought name of the killer but offered more insight into his psyche, revealing a man who relished in the notoriety and fear he generated. The persistence in solving these codes underscores the enduring allure of the

Zodiac case and the hope that future breakthroughs might still be possible.

The legacy of the Zodiac Killer is a complex tapestry of fear, fascination, and frustration. His ability to evade capture, despite leaving a trail of evidence and taunts, has cemented his place in the annals of criminal history. The case challenges our understanding of criminal behavior and the nature of evil, posing questions that remain unanswered. It also highlights the evolution of investigative techniques, from the reliance on eyewitness accounts and media engagement in the past to the modern emphasis on forensic evidence and digital analysis.

For those who continue to study the Zodiac case, it serves as a reminder of the tenacity required to pursue justice in the face of daunting obstacles. It is a testament to the enduring human spirit that seeks to unravel the mysteries of the past, driven by a desire for truth and closure. As the world changes and technology advances, there remains hope that the cipher of fear left by the Zodiac Killer will one day be fully decoded, bringing resolution to one of history's most chilling puzzles.

The Black Dahlia: Hollywood's Darkest Secret

Los Angeles, the city of dreams and illusions, became the backdrop for one of the most infamous unsolved murders in American history. On January 15, 1947, the lifeless body of Elizabeth Short was discovered in a vacant lot in Leimert Park, brutally mutilated and posed. The press quickly dubbed her "The Black Dahlia," a name inspired by her dark hair and rumored penchant for black attire, as well as a play on a popular movie title of the time. The case captured the public's imagination, intertwining with the glamour and grit of post-war Hollywood.

Elizabeth Short's life was marked by aspirations and struggle. Born in Boston in 1924, she sought to escape her troubled family life by moving to California, where she dreamed of becoming a starlet. Like many young women of her era, her journey was fraught with challenges. She navigated the transient and often perilous world of Hollywood, working various jobs and relying on the kindness of acquaintances to get by. Her striking looks and enigmatic presence left an impression on those she met, yet her life remained one of unfulfilled dreams and fleeting relationships.

The discovery of Short's body was a scene of horror that shocked even seasoned investigators. Her body had been severed at the waist, drained of blood, and meticulously cleaned. The precision of the mutilation suggested a level of surgical skill that bewildered law enforcement. The gruesome nature of the crime, combined with her youthful beauty and the sensationalist press coverage, propelled the case into the national spotlight. The mystery of who could commit such an atrocity and why became an obsession for the public and the police alike.

The investigation into Short's murder was one of the most extensive in the Los Angeles Police Department's history. Hundreds of suspects were interviewed, and numerous confessions, both genuine and false, were scrutinized. However, the lack of concrete evidence and the chaotic nature of the investigation led to a series of dead ends. The press played a significant role in shaping public perception, often sensationalizing details and perpetuating myths about Short's life and character. This media frenzy complicated the investigation, making it difficult to discern fact from fiction.

One of the primary challenges in solving the Black Dahlia case was the transient lifestyle Short led. She moved frequently, had numerous acquaintances, and left little in the way of a paper trail. This lack of stability made it difficult for investigators to piece together a coherent timeline of her final days. Additionally, the post-war atmosphere in Los Angeles, with its influx of people and burgeoning entertainment industry, created an environment of anonymity and opportunity for those with nefarious intentions.

Several suspects emerged over the years, each with varying degrees of plausibility. One of the most intriguing was Dr. George Hodel, a physician with a history of scandal and connections to the Hollywood elite. Hodel's son, Steve, a former LAPD homicide detective, later accused his father of the murder, citing evidence from his own investigation. This theory gained traction due to Hodel's medical background, which could explain the surgical nature of the crime. However, despite the compelling narrative, definitive proof linking Hodel to the murder remains elusive.

Other suspects included figures from Short's social circle and transient acquaintances she encountered in her quest for stardom. The possibility of a connection to organized crime or a spurned lover was also considered, yet none of these leads resulted in a conviction. The case remains an open wound in the annals of unsolved crimes, a reflection of the dark underbelly of a city that thrives on dreams and deception.

The legacy of the Black Dahlia extends beyond the gruesome details of the crime itself. It serves as a cautionary tale about the dangers faced by those who seek fame and fortune in a world that often values appearance over substance. The case highlights the vulnerability of young women in a society that can be both all-consuming and indifferent. It also underscores the challenges faced by law enforcement in an era before modern forensic technology and investigative techniques.

In recent years, advances in DNA analysis and digital archiving have offered new avenues for exploration. Cold case units continue to revisit the evidence, hoping that technological advancements might yield new insights. While the prospect of solving the case remains uncertain, the continued interest in the Black Dahlia reflects a broader fascination with the intersection of crime, celebrity, and human nature.

For those who study the Black Dahlia case, it is a story of ambition and tragedy, a reminder of the fragile line between aspiration and exploitation. It invites us to consider the societal forces that shape our perceptions of beauty, success, and morality. As long as the case remains unsolved, it will continue to captivate those who seek to understand the complexities of the human psyche and the shadows that lurk beneath the surface of the American dream.

In the end, the Black Dahlia is more than a murder mystery; it is a symbol of the dreams and dangers inherent in the pursuit of fame. It challenges us to confront the realities of a world where the quest for recognition can lead to unforeseen consequences. As the story of Elizabeth Short endures, it serves as a poignant reminder of the enduring power of mystery to captivate and confound, urging us to look beyond the headlines and into the heart of a city that guards its secrets well.

The Case of D.B. Cooper: The Skyjacker Who Disappeared

A crisp autumn afternoon in 1971 set the stage for one of the most audacious and perplexing mysteries in American history. It was November 24, the day before Thanksgiving, when a man using the alias "Dan Cooper" boarded Northwest Orient Airlines Flight 305 in Portland, Oregon. This seemingly ordinary passenger, later misidentified as "D.B. Cooper" by the press, would become an enigmatic figure in the annals of aviation and criminal lore. His daring hijacking and subsequent disappearance have continued to confound authorities, inspire countless theories, and capture the imagination of the public.

Dressed in a dark suit and tie, Cooper appeared unassuming as he took his seat near the rear of the plane. He ordered a bourbon and soda, and once the flight was airborne, he handed a note to the flight attendant. At first, she assumed it was merely a flirtatious gesture and tucked it away without reading. Cooper leaned toward her and whispered, "Miss, you'd better look at that note. I have a bomb." The message was clear and chilling: Cooper demanded $200,000 in cash, four parachutes, and a fuel truck standing by in Seattle for refueling. The life of everyone on board depended on the compliance of the airline and authorities.

The flight crew and passengers remained largely unaware of the hijacking, as the pilot discreetly informed air traffic control of the situation. An emergency landing was arranged at Seattle-Tacoma International Airport, while the FBI and local law enforcement scrambled to meet Cooper's demands. Upon landing, the ransom money and parachutes were delivered, and

Cooper released all 36 passengers. With only the crew remaining, the plane took off again, this time heading toward Mexico City, as per Cooper's instructions.

What transpired next would cement Cooper's place in history as a master of mystery. Somewhere over the dense forests of the Pacific Northwest, Cooper made his move. He lowered the rear stairway of the Boeing 727 and, with the ransom money strapped to his body, leapt into the night. The plane continued its flight, none the wiser as to the fate of its hijacker. By the time it landed in Reno, Nevada, Cooper had vanished, leaving behind only a few ties to reality—a black clip-on tie and a mother-of-pearl tie clip.

The ensuing search for Cooper was one of the most extensive in FBI history, yet it yielded little more than speculation and dead ends. The rugged terrain of the suspected jump zone posed significant challenges, and the cold, dark conditions on the night of the jump would have tested even the most seasoned parachutist. Despite these obstacles, no trace of Cooper was found in the immediate aftermath. The case quickly became a media sensation, with the public captivated by the hijacker's daring escape and the mystery of his whereabouts.

Over the years, the investigation into D.B. Cooper's disappearance has taken on a life of its own, spawning a multitude of theories and suspects. Some believe Cooper perished in the jump, succumbing to the harsh conditions or losing his life in the dense wilderness. Others maintain he survived, living out the rest of his days under a new identity. The FBI pursued numerous leads, investigating potential suspects and following up on tips, but none proved conclusive.

One of the most intriguing developments came in 1980, when a young boy discovered a decaying package containing $5,800 in cash along the Columbia River, a portion of the ransom money given to Cooper. This find reignited interest in the case and fueled speculation that Cooper had indeed survived the jump. However, the discovery raised more questions than it answered, particularly regarding how the money ended up miles away from the original search area.

Various individuals have been proposed as potential candidates for Cooper's true identity. Among them, Richard Floyd McCoy, a Vietnam veteran and experienced skydiver, was considered a strong suspect due to his involvement in a similar hijacking the following year. However, key differences in modus operandi and physical appearance cast doubt on this theory. Another suspect, Duane Weber, allegedly confessed to being Cooper on his deathbed, but subsequent investigations failed to substantiate the claim.

The allure of the D.B. Cooper case lies not only in the daring nature of the crime but also in the cultural impact it has had over the decades. Cooper's escape has been romanticized in books, films, and songs, symbolizing a rebellious spirit and an enduring mystery. The case challenges our understanding of criminal behavior and the limits of human ingenuity, inviting us to ponder the possibilities of escape and reinvention.

Despite the official closure of the case by the FBI in 2016, the legend of D.B. Cooper endures. Amateur sleuths, historians, and enthusiasts continue to explore the mystery, driven by a desire to solve one of the greatest puzzles of the 20th century. The case serves as a reminder of the complexities of human nature and the tantalizing allure of the unknown.

As we examine the case of D.B. Cooper, we are drawn to the questions that remain unanswered: Could one man truly outwit the authorities and disappear without a trace? What motivated his actions, and what became of him after that fateful night? These questions linger in the public consciousness, a testament to the enduring fascination with a man who leaped into the void and left the world to wonder at his fate.

In the end, the case of D.B. Cooper is more than a tale of crime and escape; it is a reflection of the human desire for adventure and mystery. It challenges us to explore the boundaries of possibility and to consider the lengths to which one might go in pursuit of freedom. As long as the mystery remains unsolved, it will continue to captivate and inspire, urging us to look beyond the ordinary and embrace the extraordinary potential of the human spirit.

JonBenét Ramsey: A Child Beauty Queen's Tragic End

On a frigid Boxing Day morning in 1996, the city of Boulder, Colorado, awoke to the shocking news of a crime that would grip the nation for decades. Inside an opulent home, adorned with festive decorations, the lifeless body of six-year-old JonBenét Ramsey was discovered by her father in the basement, sparking a media frenzy and a controversial investigation that still haunts the public consciousness.

JonBenét, a child beauty pageant star, was reported missing by her mother, Patsy Ramsey, early that same day after finding a bizarre ransom note demanding $118,000 for her return. The note, curiously specific and written on paper from within the house, immediately raised suspicions. As police arrived on the scene, the investigation began to unravel amid a series of missteps and complications that would plague the case for years to come.

The Ramsey home, a sprawling residence in an affluent neighborhood, quickly became a chaotic hub of activity. Friends and family members arrived to console the distraught parents, inadvertently contaminating the crime scene. The police, unprepared for such a high-profile case, failed to secure the premises effectively, resulting in the loss of crucial evidence. This early mishandling set the stage for the complex and contentious investigation that followed.

From the outset, the case was steeped in controversy. The ransom note, an unusual and lengthy document, appeared to be a critical piece of evidence. Written in a disjointed style with phrases borrowed from popular films, it was both theatrical and perplexing. Handwriting analysis failed to yield definitive results, though it was determined to have likely been composed by a right-handed individual. This finding, coupled with the peculiar nature of the note, led investigators to suspect someone close to the family.

As the investigation progressed, the media circus surrounding the case intensified. JonBenét's image, captured in glamorous pageant attire, was plastered across television screens and newspapers, fueling public fascination and speculation. The relentless coverage, often sensationalist in nature, influenced public perception and contributed to the pressure on law enforcement to deliver results. This scrutiny, however, also exacerbated tensions between the police and the Ramsey family, who were initially cooperative but later became wary of the investigation's direction.

Theories regarding JonBenét's murder abounded, ranging from accusations against her parents and brother to the possibility of an intruder. The family, particularly Patsy and John Ramsey, faced intense public suspicion, with many questioning their behavior in the aftermath of the crime. Yet, despite the scrutiny and a grand jury investigation, no charges were filed against them. The Ramseys consistently maintained their innocence, citing the presence of an intruder as the most plausible explanation for their daughter's death.

Among the evidence supporting the intruder theory were unidentified footprints in the snow outside the house and an open basement window, suggesting a possible point of entry. Additionally, a partial DNA profile obtained from JonBenét's clothing did not match any family members or known suspects, further complicating the narrative. Despite these findings, critics argued that the intruder theory was improbable given the lack of forced entry and the intimate knowledge of the household displayed by the perpetrator.

In the years following JonBenét's murder, advances in forensic technology provided new avenues for investigation. DNA analysis, in particular, became a focal point, with hopes that it might finally unravel the mystery. In 2008, the Boulder District Attorney's office issued a public apology to the Ramsey family, clearing them of suspicion based on newly analyzed DNA evidence. However, the case remained unsolved, and the question of who killed JonBenét lingered.

The enduring fascination with JonBenét's murder can be attributed to the confluence of factors surrounding the case:

the high-profile nature of the Ramsey family, the unsettling juxtaposition of innocence and violence, and the myriad of unanswered questions. The case has inspired numerous documentaries, books, and television specials, each offering its own interpretation and analysis. For some, it serves as a cautionary tale about the dangers of media sensationalism and the pitfalls of a flawed investigation. For others, it is a haunting reminder of the vulnerability of children and the darkness that can lurk beneath the surface of seemingly idyllic lives.

Despite the passage of time, interest in JonBenét's case remains steadfast. New theories and suspects continue to emerge, driven by amateur sleuths and professional investigators alike. The advent of social media has provided a platform for renewed discussion and debate, as well as the potential for fresh leads. Yet, despite these efforts, the truth remains elusive, locked away in the shadows of a cold winter's night.

For those who seek to understand the complexities of this case, it serves as a poignant study of the interplay between crime, media, and public perception. It challenges us to consider the impact of societal pressures on the pursuit of justice and the ways in which personal biases can shape investigative outcomes. Ultimately, JonBenét's story is one of tragedy and mystery, a reflection of the human desire for answers and the enduring quest for truth.

In our search for resolution, we are reminded of the importance of compassion and empathy, not only for the victims and their families but for all those touched by the ripples of violence. JonBenét Ramsey's legacy is one that transcends the confines of her brief life, leaving an indelible mark on the collective consciousness and a call to never forget the innocence lost amid the clamor for justice.

The Enduring Enigma of Other High-Profile Cases

Throughout history, certain high-profile cases have captured public attention and become enduring enigmas, not merely because of their complexity but due to the profound mysteries that they present. These cases often reflect broader societal issues, revealing insights into human behavior, justice, and the media's role in shaping narratives. By examining some of these enduring mysteries, we gain an understanding of why they linger in the collective consciousness and how they continue to influence discussions about crime and justice.

One such case is the disappearance of Madeleine McCann, a three-year-old British girl who vanished from a holiday apartment in Praia da Luz, Portugal, in 2007. Despite extensive investigations by both Portuguese authorities and Scotland Yard, her whereabouts remain unknown. The case has generated massive media coverage, with every development scrutinized in the tabloids and on television. The McCann case is emblematic of the challenges faced when a high-profile investigation takes place in the public eye. While the global attention has kept the case alive, it has also led to sensationalism and speculation, often complicating the pursuit of truth.

The disappearance of Malaysia Airlines Flight MH370 in 2014 is another modern mystery that has confounded investigators and the public alike. The flight vanished en route from Kuala Lumpur to Beijing with 239 passengers and crew on board, leaving behind a trail of unanswered questions. Extensive searches have yielded little more than fragments of the aircraft, leading to numerous theories about what might have happened. The case highlights the limitations of technology and the vastness of the world's oceans, reminding us of the fragility of modern life and the unresolved mysteries that can arise even in an age of advanced technology.

The case of the Somerton Man, also known as the Tamam Shud case, is a mystery that dates back to 1948 in Australia. An unidentified man was found dead on Somerton Beach near Adelaide, with no identification and a scrap of paper bearing the Persian phrase "Tamam Shud" (meaning "ended" or "finished") in his pocket. Despite extensive investigations, his identity and the circumstances of his death remain unknown. The case has intrigued amateur sleuths and professional detectives for decades, inspiring theories ranging from espionage to an elaborate suicide. This enigma underscores the enduring appeal of unsolved cases and the human fascination with the unknown.

The Zodiac Killer, whose reign of terror in the late 1960s and early 1970s has been the subject of numerous investigations and cultural depictions, remains one of the most infamous unsolved serial killer cases in American history. The killer's cryptic letters and ciphers sent to newspapers taunted law enforcement and captivated the public, creating an aura of mystery that has persisted for decades. Despite numerous suspects and extensive investigations, the Zodiac's identity remains a mystery. The case serves as a reminder of the challenges faced by law enforcement in dealing with highly intelligent and elusive criminals, as well as the lasting impact that such cases can have on popular culture.

These high-profile cases share common themes that contribute to their enduring intrigue. They involve elements of mystery, a lack of closure, and often a significant amount of public and media attention. The role of the media in these cases cannot be understated, as it shapes public perception and can influence the direction of investigations. The intense scrutiny can sometimes hinder the search for truth, as speculation and sensationalism overshadow objective analysis.

The fascination with these cases also stems from their reflection of societal fears and anxieties. Disappearances, unsolved murders, and unexplained phenomena tap into deep-seated fears of the unknown and uncontrollable. They challenge our understanding of the world and our place in it, prompting us to question the nature of justice and the limits of human knowledge. These cases remind us that despite advances in technology and investigative methods, some mysteries may remain unsolved, leaving us to ponder the complexities of human nature and the universe.

Efforts to solve these cases continue, driven by advances in forensic science, digital technology, and global communication networks. Cold case units and dedicated amateur investigators tirelessly pursue new leads, hoping to shed light on these enduring enigmas. The potential for resolution remains, as new evidence or breakthroughs could emerge at any time, offering hope to those seeking answers.

For those who study these high-profile cases, they offer a window into the human psyche and the dynamics of crime and justice in a rapidly changing world. They challenge us to consider the impact of media and public perception on the search for truth and to reflect on our own fascination with the macabre and mysterious. As these cases continue to capture the public's imagination, they serve as a testament to the enduring power of mystery and the human desire for resolution.

In examining these enduring enigmas, we are reminded of the importance of critical thinking, empathy, and perseverance in the face of uncertainty. These cases invite us to engage with the complexities of the human experience and to seek understanding in a world where not all questions have answers. As long as these mysteries remain unsolved, they will continue to inspire curiosity and debate, urging us to explore the boundaries of knowledge and the depths of our own humanity.

Chapter 4: The Role of Forensic Science in Cold Cases

Advances in DNA Technology and Its Impact

The evolution of DNA technology has profoundly transformed the landscape of forensic science and criminal investigation. Its impact on solving cold cases, exonerating the innocent, and securing convictions for the guilty cannot be overstated. From humble beginnings in the mid-1980s, when DNA profiling first emerged as a groundbreaking tool, this technology has advanced in ways that have reshaped the justice system and offered new hope for resolving long-standing mysteries.

The story of DNA technology began with the pioneering work of Sir Alec Jeffreys, who, in 1984, developed a technique for identifying individuals based on unique patterns in their DNA. This breakthrough laid the foundation for DNA profiling, a method that quickly proved invaluable in forensic investigations. The first notable application of DNA evidence in a criminal case was in 1986, when it was used to convict Colin Pitchfork of the murder of two young girls in England. This landmark case demonstrated the potential of DNA technology to provide irrefutable evidence and set the stage for its widespread adoption.

As DNA technology advanced, so too did its applications in criminal justice. The establishment of DNA databases, such as the Combined DNA Index System (CODIS) in the United States, allowed for the storage and comparison of DNA profiles on a national scale. This development enabled law enforcement agencies to link crimes and identify suspects with unprecedented efficiency. Cold cases, long considered unsolvable, were reopened with the hope that new DNA evidence might provide the missing piece of the puzzle. In many instances, these efforts have led to the resolution of cases that had remained dormant for decades, bringing closure to victims' families and communities.

One of the most significant impacts of DNA technology has been its role in exonerating the wrongfully convicted. Organizations like the Innocence Project have leveraged DNA evidence to challenge wrongful convictions, shining a light on the fallibility of traditional investigative methods and the potential for human error in the justice system. Since the advent of DNA testing, hundreds of individuals who were wrongfully imprisoned have been freed, highlighting the importance of this technology in ensuring justice and preventing miscarriages of justice.

The precision and reliability of DNA evidence have also bolstered the prosecution of violent crimes. In cases involving sexual assault, for example, DNA profiles can conclusively link a suspect to a victim, providing compelling evidence in court. This has not only increased conviction rates but has also acted as a deterrent to potential offenders, who are now more aware of the likelihood of being caught due to DNA analysis. The ripple effect of this technology extends beyond individual cases, contributing to a broader sense of security and trust in the justice system.

However, the rapid advancement of DNA technology has also raised ethical and privacy concerns. The creation and expansion of DNA databases have led to debates about the balance between public safety and individual privacy rights. Critics argue that the retention of DNA profiles, particularly those of individuals who have not been convicted of a crime, poses a risk of misuse and could lead to unwarranted surveillance. These concerns underscore the need for robust legal frameworks and oversight to ensure that the benefits of DNA technology are realized without compromising civil liberties.

The potential of DNA technology continues to grow, driven by ongoing innovations and research. Techniques such as next-generation sequencing and familial DNA searching have expanded the scope of forensic analysis, enabling investigators to glean more information from smaller and degraded samples. These advancements hold promise for solving even the most challenging cases, where traditional methods have fallen short.

Familial DNA searching, in particular, has emerged as a powerful tool for identifying suspects when direct matches are unavailable. By analyzing genetic similarities between profiles, investigators can identify potential relatives of a suspect, narrowing the field of inquiry and providing new leads. This method has been instrumental in solving high-profile cases, such as the identification of the Golden State Killer, a notorious serial offender whose crimes spanned decades. The success of this approach has demonstrated the potential of DNA technology to uncover hidden connections and bring long-sought justice to victims and their families.

Despite its transformative impact, the use of DNA technology is not without its challenges. The interpretation of complex DNA mixtures, the potential for contamination, and the reliance on statistical probabilities in analysis require a high degree of expertise and precision. Forensic scientists must navigate these complexities to ensure the integrity and accuracy of their findings, underscoring the importance of rigorous training and standardization in the field.

As DNA technology continues to evolve, it is crucial for the legal and scientific communities to collaborate in addressing the ethical, legal, and technical challenges that arise. This collaboration will be essential in maintaining public confidence in the justice system and ensuring that DNA evidence is used responsibly and effectively.

For those entering the field of forensic science or criminal investigation, understanding the capabilities and limitations of DNA technology is paramount. By staying informed about the latest advancements and maintaining a commitment to ethical practices, practitioners can harness the power of DNA analysis to make meaningful contributions to the pursuit of justice.

In reflecting on the journey of DNA technology, we are reminded of its profound impact on society and the justice system. It serves as a testament to the power of scientific innovation to drive positive change and underscores the importance of vigilance and integrity in its application. As we look to the future, the continued evolution of DNA technology promises to unlock new possibilities, offering hope for the resolution of even the most enduring mysteries.

The Evolution of Crime Scene Investigation Techniques

Crime scene investigation has undergone significant transformation over the years, evolving from rudimentary methods to sophisticated techniques that harness cutting-edge technology. This evolution has been driven by the need for precision, accuracy, and the increasing complexity of crime itself. Understanding this progression offers valuable insights into the challenges and innovations that have shaped modern forensic science and the meticulous art of crime scene investigation.

In the early days of forensic science, crime scene investigation relied heavily on the keen observational skills of detectives and investigators. The primary focus was on gathering physical evidence that could be seen with the naked eye—such as weapons, footprints, and bloodstains. Investigators meticulously documented the scene through sketches and notes, attempting to reconstruct the sequence of events. However, the process was often subjective and prone to human error, with limited tools at their disposal to analyze the evidence thoroughly.

The late 19th and early 20th centuries marked the beginning of a more scientific approach to crime scene investigation. The introduction of fingerprint analysis revolutionized the field, providing a reliable method for identifying individuals based on unique patterns in their fingerprints. This breakthrough laid the groundwork for the development of more advanced techniques, as the law enforcement community recognized the potential of scientific methods in solving crimes.

As forensic science gained momentum, new techniques emerged, each contributing to a more comprehensive understanding of crime scenes. The advent of trace evidence analysis, for example, allowed investigators to examine minute particles such as hair, fibers, and soil, which could provide critical links between a suspect and a crime scene. The meticulous collection and examination of these traces underscored the importance of preserving the integrity of the crime scene, as even the smallest piece of evidence could yield significant insights.

The mid-20th century saw the rise of forensic chemistry and toxicology, further expanding the capabilities of crime scene investigators. Advances in chemical analysis enabled the detection of substances such as drugs, poisons, and explosives, providing crucial evidence in cases involving drug-related crimes, poisoning, and bombings. These developments highlighted the interdisciplinary nature of forensic science, as investigators increasingly collaborated with chemists, biologists, and other specialists to solve complex cases.

One of the most transformative advancements in crime scene investigation has been the integration of DNA analysis. Since its introduction in the 1980s, DNA technology has become an indispensable tool in forensic science, offering unparalleled accuracy in identifying individuals. The ability to extract and analyze DNA from biological samples such as blood, saliva, and hair has revolutionized the way investigators approach crime scenes, enabling them to link suspects to crimes with a high degree of certainty. DNA evidence has not only helped solve countless cases but has also played a pivotal role in exonerating individuals wrongfully convicted of crimes.

The digital age has ushered in a new era of crime scene investigation, characterized by the use of advanced technology and data analysis. Digital forensics, for instance, involves the extraction and examination of data from electronic devices such as computers, smartphones, and security cameras. This field has become increasingly important as cybercrime and digital evidence play a larger role in criminal investigations. The ability to recover deleted files, trace online activities, and analyze digital footprints has opened up new avenues for solving crimes in the digital realm.

In addition to digital forensics, the use of 3D scanning and imaging technology has enhanced the documentation and analysis of crime scenes. These tools allow investigators to create detailed, accurate representations of crime scenes, preserving them in digital form for future analysis and courtroom presentations. This technology not only improves the accuracy of crime scene reconstructions but also facilitates collaboration among investigators, experts, and legal professionals by providing a clear, visual representation of the evidence.

Despite these advancements, crime scene investigation remains a highly demanding and meticulous process. The principles of careful documentation, preservation of evidence, and methodical analysis continue to be the bedrock of successful investigations. Investigators must remain vigilant in their efforts to avoid contamination and ensure the integrity of the evidence, as even the most advanced technology cannot compensate for compromised samples.

For those entering the field of crime scene investigation, a deep understanding of both traditional and modern techniques is essential. Training programs emphasize the importance of attention to detail, critical thinking, and the ability to adapt to new technologies and methodologies. As the field continues to evolve, investigators must be prepared to integrate new tools and approaches into their work while maintaining the highest standards of ethical and professional conduct.

The evolution of crime scene investigation techniques reflects the dynamic nature of forensic science and the ongoing quest for greater accuracy and reliability in solving crimes. Each advancement builds upon the knowledge and experience of previous generations, driving the field forward and enhancing our ability to uncover the truth. As technology continues to advance, the future of crime scene investigation holds the promise of even more sophisticated tools and techniques, offering new opportunities to bring justice to victims and their families.

In looking back at the journey of crime scene investigation, we see a testament to human ingenuity and the relentless pursuit of knowledge. The field has come a long way from its humble beginnings, and yet, the core mission remains unchanged: to uncover the truth and ensure justice is served. By embracing innovation and adhering to the principles of rigorous scientific inquiry, crime scene investigators will continue to play a crucial role in the fight against crime, adapting to new challenges and opportunities with each passing decade.

Digital Forensics and Uncovering New Leads

In the ever-evolving landscape of modern crime, digital forensics has emerged as an indispensable tool in the investigator's arsenal, offering new avenues to uncover leads and solve cases. As technology has become integral to daily life, it has also become a fertile ground for criminal activities, necessitating a specialized approach to extracting and analyzing digital evidence. This chapter delves into the world of digital forensics, exploring its methodologies, challenges, and the transformative impact it has on criminal investigations.

Digital forensics is the science of retrieving and analyzing data from electronic devices to uncover evidence relevant to criminal investigations. This encompasses a wide range of digital media, including computers, smartphones, tablets, external hard drives, and even smart devices such as home assistants and wearable technology. The digital trail left behind by individuals can be extensive, and when properly harnessed, it provides invaluable insights into criminal behavior and connections.

The process of digital forensics begins with the identification and preservation of digital evidence. Ensuring that data is not altered or corrupted during retrieval is crucial, as the integrity of the evidence is paramount for it to be admissible in court. Forensic experts employ specialized tools and techniques to create a bit-by-bit copy of the data, known as a forensic image, which allows them to analyze the evidence without affecting the original device. This meticulous process is akin to preserving a crime scene, where care is taken to maintain the authenticity and reliability of the evidence.

Once the evidence is preserved, forensic analysts delve into the data, seeking clues that can shed light on the case at hand. This may involve examining communication logs, such as emails, text messages, and social media interactions, which can reveal relationships, motives, and alibis. In cases of financial fraud, analysts may trace transactions and access records to uncover patterns of illicit activity. The sheer volume of data that can be extracted from digital devices is staggering, requiring sophisticated software and analytical skills to sift through and identify pertinent information.

One of the most powerful aspects of digital forensics is its ability to recover deleted data. Contrary to popular belief, deleting a file does not permanently erase it from a device. Instead, it merely removes the file's reference from the system's directory, leaving the data intact until it is overwritten. Forensic tools can often retrieve these "deleted" files, providing critical evidence that suspects believed to be erased. This capability has proven instrumental in numerous investigations, where recovered data has led to new leads and breakthroughs.

In the realm of cybercrime, digital forensics plays an even more prominent role. Cybercriminals exploit the anonymity of the internet to conduct a range of illicit activities, from hacking and identity theft to the distribution of illegal content. Digital forensics enables investigators to trace the origins of cyberattacks, identify perpetrators, and gather evidence for prosecution. Techniques such as IP address tracking, network traffic analysis, and malware reverse engineering are employed to unravel the complex web of cybercrime.

Despite its efficacy, digital forensics is not without its challenges. The rapid pace of technological advancement means that forensic experts must constantly update their knowledge and tools to keep pace with new devices, operating systems, and encryption methods. The increasing prevalence of encryption and data protection measures poses additional hurdles, as gaining access to encrypted data can be a time-consuming and technically demanding process. Furthermore, the global nature of digital evidence often necessitates cross-jurisdictional collaboration, adding layers of complexity to investigations.

Legal and ethical considerations also play a significant role in digital forensics. The collection and analysis of digital evidence must adhere to strict legal standards to ensure that individuals' privacy rights are respected and that the evidence is admissible in court. This requires a delicate balance between investigative needs and civil liberties, underscoring the importance of clear legal frameworks and guidelines.

For beginners entering the field of digital forensics, a strong foundation in computer science and information technology is essential. Familiarity with various operating systems, programming languages, and cybersecurity principles will provide the necessary technical skills to navigate the complexities of digital investigations. Additionally, developing strong analytical and problem-solving abilities is crucial, as forensic analysts must be able to interpret data, identify patterns, and draw meaningful conclusions from digital evidence.

Training and education in digital forensics typically encompass a combination of theoretical knowledge and practical experience. Many institutions offer dedicated programs and certifications in digital forensics, providing students with hands-on experience in forensic labs and simulations. Staying abreast of the latest developments in technology and forensic techniques is also vital, as the field is constantly evolving.

The impact of digital forensics on criminal investigations is profound, offering new opportunities to uncover leads and solve cases that might otherwise remain unsolved. By leveraging digital evidence, investigators can piece together narratives, establish timelines, and connect dots that were previously invisible. The digital footprints left behind by suspects provide a rich tapestry of information that, when skillfully analyzed, can lead to the resolution of even the most complex cases.

In reflecting on the role of digital forensics, it is clear that this discipline is not just about technology—it is about people. The data extracted from digital devices tells stories about human behavior, relationships, and choices. By understanding and interpreting these narratives, forensic analysts contribute to the pursuit of justice and the protection of society.

As technology continues to evolve, so too will the field of digital forensics. The challenges and opportunities presented by new devices, data types, and cyber threats will shape the future of investigations, demanding innovation, adaptability, and a commitment to ethical practices. For those dedicated to the pursuit of truth in the digital age, digital forensics offers a dynamic and rewarding path, where the quest for knowledge and justice intersect.

The   Challenges   of   Reanalyzing   Old   Evidence

Reanalyzing old evidence is a critical process that can breathe new life into cold cases and long-standing mysteries. This endeavor, however, is fraught with challenges that require meticulous attention to detail, advanced technology, and a thorough understanding of the historical and contextual nuances of the evidence involved. As investigators revisit these cases, they must navigate a complex landscape of scientific, legal, and ethical considerations to ensure that justice is served.

One of the primary challenges in reanalyzing old evidence is the degradation of materials over time. Biological samples, such as blood and tissue, can deteriorate due to environmental conditions, mishandling, or the mere passage of time. This degradation can compromise the integrity of the evidence, making it difficult to extract reliable data. Advances in forensic technology, such as improved DNA extraction methods and more sensitive analytical techniques, have made it possible to glean information from degraded samples that were once thought unusable. However, the success of these methods is not guaranteed, and investigators must approach each case with a careful assessment of the sample's condition and potential for yielding viable results.

Another significant hurdle is the chain of custody and documentation associated with old evidence. In many cases, records from past investigations may be incomplete, inaccurate, or missing altogether. Maintaining a clear and unbroken chain of custody is essential for ensuring the admissibility of evidence in court. Investigators must painstakingly reconstruct this chain, often relying on archival materials, interviews with retired personnel, and other historical sources to verify the provenance and handling of the evidence. This process requires a keen eye for detail and an understanding of the historical context in which the original investigation was conducted.

The reanalysis of old evidence also necessitates a reevaluation of the forensic methods and techniques used in the original investigation. Forensic science has evolved significantly over the decades, with new methodologies and technologies supplanting older, less reliable ones. Investigators must critically assess whether the original conclusions drawn from the evidence were based on sound scientific principles or if they require reevaluation in light of contemporary standards. This reevaluation can be a delicate process, as it may challenge established narratives and force a reconsideration of past judicial outcomes.

Legal considerations play a pivotal role in reanalyzing old evidence. The admissibility of new findings in court hinges on the ability to demonstrate that the reanalysis was conducted using accepted scientific methods and that the evidence has been preserved in a condition that ensures its reliability. Legal teams must work closely with forensic experts to develop a robust strategy for presenting new evidence, addressing potential challenges from opposing counsel, and ensuring that the rights of all parties involved are respected. This collaboration is essential for navigating the complex legal landscape and achieving a just outcome.

Ethical considerations are equally important in the reanalysis of old evidence. Investigators must balance the pursuit of truth with the potential impact on individuals and communities affected by the case. The reopening of old cases can stir up emotional and psychological distress for victims' families, suspects, and witnesses. It is crucial for investigators to approach these cases with sensitivity, transparency, and a commitment to ethical standards that prioritize the well-being of all involved.

Despite these challenges, the reanalysis of old evidence offers significant opportunities for resolving cold cases and achieving justice. Technological advancements, such as enhanced DNA profiling techniques and digital forensics, have opened new avenues for uncovering evidence that was previously inaccessible. These innovations allow investigators to identify new leads, corroborate existing findings, and, in some cases, exonerate individuals who were wrongfully convicted.

For those entering the field of forensic investigation, understanding the intricacies of reanalyzing old evidence is vital. This process requires a multidisciplinary approach, drawing on expertise in forensic science, legal principles, historical research, and ethical considerations. Training programs should emphasize the importance of collaboration, critical thinking, and adaptability, equipping investigators with the skills and knowledge necessary to tackle the unique challenges presented by old evidence.

In practice, reanalyzing old evidence involves a methodical and systematic approach. Investigators must begin by thoroughly reviewing the case file, identifying gaps in the original investigation, and prioritizing evidence for reanalysis. This process often involves consulting with experts in various forensic disciplines to determine the most appropriate methods for reexamining each piece of evidence. Throughout the process, maintaining meticulous records and documentation is essential for ensuring the integrity and admissibility of the findings.

The potential impact of successful reanalysis is profound. Solving cold cases provides closure to victims' families, restores public confidence in the justice system, and deters future criminal activity by demonstrating that justice can be achieved, even after many years. Moreover, the insights gained from reanalyzing old evidence contribute to the ongoing advancement of forensic science, informing best practices and guiding future investigations.

As technology and forensic methodologies continue to evolve, the reanalysis of old evidence will remain a dynamic and challenging field. Investigators must remain vigilant in their pursuit of truth, embracing innovation while adhering to the highest standards of scientific rigor and ethical conduct. By doing so, they can unlock the potential of old evidence to illuminate the past and pave the way for a more just and equitable future.

The journey of reanalyzing old evidence is a testament to the enduring power of forensic science and the relentless pursuit of justice. It reminds us that every piece of evidence, no matter how old or degraded, holds the potential to reveal new truths and change lives. As investigators confront the challenges of this process, they carry forward a legacy of dedication, resilience, and hope, striving to ensure that no case is ever truly closed until justice is served.

Case Studies of Forensic Breakthroughs

The annals of forensic science are peppered with remarkable breakthroughs that have not only solved complex cases but have also propelled the field forward. These pivotal moments, often arising from innovative thinking and the application of cutting-edge technology, have demonstrated the power of forensic science to illuminate the truth and deliver justice. Through detailed case studies, we can appreciate the transformative impact of these breakthroughs and the lessons they offer to budding forensic experts.

One such landmark case occurred in the mid-1980s, when the small town of Narborough, England, became the epicenter of a forensic revolution. Two young girls had been brutally murdered, and despite exhaustive investigations, the police struggled to identify the perpetrator. It was in this context that Sir Alec Jeffreys, a genetics researcher at the University of Leicester, introduced the world to DNA profiling. By comparing DNA samples from the crime scenes with those of local men, the investigation ultimately led to the conviction of Colin Pitchfork, making it the first case in history to use DNA evidence to solve a crime. This breakthrough not only secured justice for the victims but also marked the dawn of DNA technology in forensic science, setting a precedent for future investigations.

Another compelling example of forensic ingenuity is the case of the BTK Killer, which spanned over three decades and left the Wichita, Kansas, community in fear. Dennis Rader, the self-named BTK Killer, taunted law enforcement with letters detailing his crimes. For years, he remained elusive, until a digital breadcrumb finally led to his downfall. In 2004, Rader sent a floppy disk to the police, believing it to be untraceable. However, forensic analysts extracted metadata from the disk, revealing a deleted Microsoft Word document that linked the disk to Rader's church. This digital forensic breakthrough, combined with DNA evidence, culminated in Rader's arrest and conviction. The case underscored the growing importance of digital forensics in contemporary investigations and highlighted the potential of seemingly innocuous digital artifacts to unravel complex cases.

Forensic breakthroughs are not confined to criminal cases alone; they have also played a crucial role in historical investigations. The mystery surrounding the identity of the infamous Romanov family, executed during the Russian Revolution, persisted for decades until forensic science offered clarity. In the 1990s, skeletal remains believed to be those of the Romanovs were discovered in a forest near Ekaterinburg. Using mitochondrial DNA analysis, scientists confirmed that the remains belonged to the Romanov family, resolving a historical enigma and providing closure to a chapter of Russian history. This case demonstrated the power of forensic techniques to address questions that transcend time, bridging the gap between past and present.

The Green River Killer investigation is another testament to the persistence of forensic science. Gary Ridgway's killing spree in Washington State during the 1980s and 1990s resulted in the deaths of dozens of women. Despite initial efforts, Ridgway remained at large, eluding capture for years. It was not until the advent of advanced DNA testing in the early 2000s that investigators could definitively link Ridgway to the crimes. By reanalyzing evidence with improved DNA techniques, authorities were able to secure Ridgway's confession and bring him to justice. This case highlighted the evolving nature of forensic science and the potential for breakthroughs to occur even years after a crime has been committed.

Forensic breakthroughs are often the result of collaboration between diverse disciplines and the application of innovative thinking. The case of the Boston Strangler, for instance, showcased the power of interdisciplinary collaboration. Albert DeSalvo's confession to the murders of several women in the Boston area was initially met with skepticism, as physical evidence was lacking. Decades later, forensic scientists used a combination of DNA analysis and genealogical research to confirm DeSalvo's involvement in the murders, providing definitive answers to a case that had long been shrouded in doubt. This case underscored the importance of integrating new methodologies and cross-disciplinary expertise in forensic investigations.

These case studies illustrate the profound impact of forensic breakthroughs on the pursuit of justice. Forensic science has the unique ability to connect disparate pieces of evidence, uncover hidden truths, and provide clarity in even the most perplexing cases. As technology and methodologies continue to advance, the potential for future breakthroughs is boundless, offering new opportunities to solve cases and deliver justice.

For those entering the field of forensic science, these case studies offer valuable lessons and inspiration. They highlight the importance of perseverance, creativity, and a willingness to embrace new technologies and approaches. Training and education in forensic science should emphasize the development of critical thinking skills, the ability to adapt to new challenges, and the importance of maintaining ethical standards in all aspects of investigation.

The stories of forensic breakthroughs serve as a testament to the power of science and human ingenuity to overcome adversity and uncover the truth. They remind us of the vital role that forensic science plays in society and the responsibility that comes with it. As forensic practitioners continue to push the boundaries of what is possible, they carry forward a legacy of innovation and dedication to justice.

In reflecting on these achievements, we are reminded that every case, no matter how daunting, holds the potential for resolution through forensic science. By learning from past successes and embracing the challenges of the future, forensic experts can continue to make meaningful contributions to the pursuit of truth and justice. The journey of forensic investigation is one of discovery and determination, a testament to the enduring quest for knowledge and the unwavering commitment to making the world a safer and more just place.

Chapter 5: The Human Element: Families, Victims, and Investigators

The Emotional Toll on Families Left in Limbo

When a loved one goes missing or falls victim to a crime, families often find themselves thrust into an agonizing state of limbo. The emotional toll this uncertainty takes is profound, affecting every facet of their lives. Unlike cases with clear resolutions, these families are left grappling with unanswered questions, enduring an endless cycle of hope and despair. Understanding this emotional landscape is crucial for those who support them, from law enforcement to mental health professionals and community members.

The initial shock of a disappearance or unresolved crime sends ripples through a family, disrupting the very fabric of their existence. There is no way to prepare for such an event, and the immediate aftermath is often characterized by disbelief and confusion. The mind struggles to comprehend the situation, clinging to the hope that it is all a misunderstanding, a temporary nightmare from which they will soon awaken. This period is marked by a frantic search for answers, as families mobilize resources to gather information, organize search parties, and engage with authorities.

Hope becomes a double-edged sword, providing the strength to continue but also prolonging the agony. Families hold on to every possibility, no matter how slim, that their loved one will return. This hope can be all-consuming, dictating daily routines and decisions. It can lead to strained relationships, as different family members cope in contrasting ways—some may cling to optimism, while others prepare for the worst. The lack of closure prevents the natural grieving process, leaving emotions suspended in a state of unresolved tension.

The passage of time compounds the emotional toll. As days turn into weeks, months, and even years, the initial surge of community support often wanes, leaving families feeling isolated and forgotten. They face the daunting task of maintaining awareness and keeping the search alive, often turning to media and social networks to keep their loved one's story in the public eye. This responsibility can be overwhelming, as they juggle the demands of maintaining normalcy in their lives while never letting go of the search.

The psychological impact of living in limbo can manifest in various ways, including anxiety, depression, and post-traumatic stress disorder (PTSD). Families may experience hyper-vigilance, constantly on edge, and seeking signs or clues. Sleep disturbances and nightmares are common, as the mind struggles to find peace amidst the turmoil. The emotional rollercoaster takes a physical toll as well, leading to exhaustion and a compromised immune system. Professional counseling and support groups can provide a lifeline, offering a space for families to share their experiences and find solace in knowing they are not alone.

Children are particularly vulnerable to the effects of living in limbo. They may struggle to understand the situation, internalizing feelings of guilt or abandonment. Their academic performance and social interactions can suffer, as the stress of the unknown weighs heavily on their young shoulders. It is essential for parents and caregivers to provide reassurance and open communication, helping children express their emotions in a healthy way. Schools and educators can play a supportive role by fostering an understanding environment and offering resources tailored to the child's needs.

The legal and investigative processes add another layer of complexity to the emotional toll. Families often find themselves navigating a labyrinth of procedures and protocols, seeking justice or answers while feeling disempowered by the system. The pace of investigations can be frustratingly slow, and the lack of regular updates can lead to feelings of helplessness and mistrust. Establishing a positive relationship with law enforcement is crucial, as it fosters collaboration and ensures that families remain informed and engaged.

Financial strain is another harsh reality for families left in limbo. The costs associated with searches, legal fees, and time taken off work can quickly deplete resources. Some families may face difficult decisions, such as selling assets or accumulating debt, to sustain their efforts. Community fundraising and nonprofit organizations can provide much-needed support, alleviating some of the financial burdens and allowing families to focus on what truly matters—the search for their loved ones.

Despite the myriad challenges, resilience often emerges as a defining characteristic of families navigating this painful journey. Many find strength in advocacy, channeling their grief into efforts to prevent similar tragedies and support others in similar situations. Advocacy can take many forms, from raising awareness and lobbying for legislative change to establishing foundations in their loved one's name. This sense of purpose can provide healing and hope, transforming personal pain into a force for positive change.

For those who support families living in limbo, empathy and understanding are paramount. It is essential to recognize the unique challenges they face and offer nonjudgmental, compassionate assistance. Whether through professional services, community initiatives, or simple acts of kindness, support networks can make a significant difference in alleviating the emotional burden and fostering resilience.

The experience of living in limbo is a profound testament to the human capacity for endurance and hope. While the journey is fraught with challenges, it also reveals the strength of the human spirit and the power of love to transcend the darkest moments. For families caught in this painful limbo, every day is a testament to their unwavering commitment to their loved ones and their refusal to give up on the possibility of a resolution.

In the face of uncertainty, these families teach us valuable lessons about the importance of empathy, community, and resilience. By understanding and supporting them, we honor their journey and contribute to a world where no family has to navigate this path alone. Through collective effort and compassion, we can help bring light to the darkness and provide hope to those who need it most.

Personal Stories of Resilience and Hope

Among the shadows of adversity, stories of resilience and hope shine brightly, illuminating the indomitable human spirit. These personal narratives, borne from challenges and trials, serve as powerful testaments to the strength and courage that reside within individuals. They inspire, uplift, and remind us that even in the darkest moments, there is a flicker of hope that can guide us through. This chapter delves into the lives of those who have faced overwhelming odds and emerged stronger, offering practical insights and inspiration for navigating life's toughest battles.

Consider the journey of Sarah, a woman whose life was upended by a devastating accident that left her paralyzed from the waist down. In an instant, her world was transformed, filled with uncertainty and fear. Yet, amid the turmoil, Sarah discovered a reservoir of resilience she never knew she possessed. Instead of succumbing to despair, she chose to focus on her rehabilitation, setting small, achievable goals that gradually restored her sense of independence and self-worth. Her story exemplifies the power of setting realistic objectives and celebrating incremental victories, highlighting the importance of patience and perseverance in the face of adversity.

Sarah's journey was not one she embarked on alone. The unwavering support of her family and friends played a crucial role in her recovery. They rallied around her, providing emotional and practical assistance, reinforcing the idea that resilience is often a collective effort. Sarah's experience underscores the value of nurturing a strong support network, one that can offer encouragement, empathy, and a sense of belonging during challenging times. For those facing similar struggles, reaching out and fostering connections can be a vital step in the healing process.

In another part of the world, we find Daniel, a young entrepreneur who faced the collapse of his business amid an economic downturn. The loss was staggering, both financially and emotionally, leaving him grappling with feelings of failure and self-doubt. Yet, rather than being defeated, Daniel saw this as an opportunity to learn and grow. He meticulously analyzed his mistakes, sought guidance from mentors, and gradually rebuilt his venture from the ground up. His story illustrates the importance of adaptability and a growth mindset, demonstrating how setbacks can serve as powerful catalysts for personal and professional development.

Daniel's resilience was fueled by his unwavering belief in his vision and the courage to take calculated risks. He embraced the uncertainty, viewing it not as a barrier but as a landscape of possibilities. This perspective shift is crucial for anyone navigating adversity; by reframing challenges as opportunities for learning and exploration, individuals can cultivate a sense of agency and empowerment. Daniel's journey also highlights the significance of mentorship and continuous learning, encouraging individuals to seek out resources and guidance to enhance their skills and knowledge.

For Maria, a survivor of a natural disaster that obliterated her home and community, resilience took on a different form. In the aftermath of the devastation, she found herself grappling with profound loss and displacement. Yet, amidst the chaos, Maria discovered a profound sense of purpose in helping others rebuild their lives. She spearheaded community initiatives, organized volunteer efforts, and advocated for resources and support. Her story reveals the transformative power of altruism and collective action, showing how acts of kindness and solidarity can foster resilience and hope in both individuals and communities.

Maria's experience underscores the notion that resilience is not merely about enduring; it is about thriving and making a positive impact despite adversity. By channeling her energy into helping others, she found a sense of meaning and fulfillment that transcended her personal loss. Her journey serves as a reminder that in times of crisis, looking beyond oneself and engaging in acts of service can cultivate a sense of connectedness and purpose, strengthening the bonds that hold communities together.

In the realm of personal relationships, resilience often manifests in the ability to navigate and heal from emotional wounds. Take the story of James and Lily, a couple who faced the betrayal of infidelity. The revelation shattered their trust, leaving them at a crossroads. Yet, through open communication, therapy, and a commitment to rebuilding their partnership, they discovered a renewed sense of intimacy and understanding. Their journey illustrates the power of forgiveness and vulnerability, emphasizing that resilience in relationships requires a willingness to confront difficult emotions and work collaboratively towards healing and growth.

James and Lily's experience highlights the importance of communication and emotional honesty in fostering resilience within relationships. By creating a safe space for dialogue and actively listening to each other's perspectives, they were able to rebuild trust and forge a deeper connection. Their story encourages individuals to approach relationship challenges with empathy and openness, recognizing that resilience often involves embracing vulnerability and the courage to forgive.

These personal stories of resilience and hope offer valuable lessons and insights for anyone facing adversity. They remind us that resilience is not a fixed trait but a dynamic process that can be cultivated and strengthened over time. By embracing the challenges we encounter, seeking support, and remaining open to growth and change, we can navigate life's trials with grace and determination.

For those beginning their journey towards resilience, it is important to remember that every path is unique. What works for one person may not work for another, and that's okay. The key is to be patient with oneself, to explore different strategies and approaches, and to remain committed to the journey. Whether it's setting small goals, seeking mentorship, engaging in acts of service, or nurturing relationships, there are countless ways to foster resilience and hope.

Ultimately, these stories remind us that adversity, while challenging, can also be a source of immense strength and transformation. By sharing our experiences and supporting one another, we can create a world where resilience and hope flourish, empowering individuals and communities to overcome even the most daunting obstacles. In the end, it is the human spirit, resilient and unyielding, that lights the way forward, illuminating the path to healing, growth, and renewal.

The Dedication of Cold Case Investigators

Cold case investigators are often the unsung heroes of the justice system, dedicating their careers to unraveling mysteries that have long since faded from the public eye. Their work is a testament to unwavering commitment, patience, and meticulous attention to detail. These professionals possess a unique blend of skills and attributes that enable them to navigate the complex and often frustrating world of unresolved cases. Their dedication not only brings closure to families but also reinforces the integrity of the justice system.

At the core of a cold case investigator's dedication is an unyielding pursuit of truth. These individuals are driven by the belief that every victim deserves justice, regardless of how much time has passed. This conviction fuels their determination to delve into cases that others might have abandoned, sifting through mountains of evidence with fresh eyes and renewed purpose. Their work often involves revisiting crime scenes, conducting new interviews, and reanalyzing old evidence using the latest forensic technologies. This meticulous approach is essential for uncovering new leads and piecing together the puzzle of a cold case.

Cold case investigators must also possess a keen analytical mind. They are trained to look beyond the obvious, identifying patterns and connections that may have been overlooked in previous investigations. This requires a deep understanding of criminal behavior, forensic science, and investigative techniques. It also demands a willingness to question assumptions and challenge preconceived notions, as the smallest detail can sometimes be the key to solving a case. Investigators must remain open-minded and adaptable, ready to explore new avenues of inquiry as they arise.

In addition to their analytical skills, cold case investigators must be adept communicators. Much of their work involves interacting with victims' families, witnesses, and other law enforcement professionals. They must be able to convey complex information clearly and compassionately, building trust and rapport with those involved in the case. This requires empathy and emotional intelligence, as the families of victims are often grappling with the pain of unresolved loss. Investigators must navigate these sensitive situations with care, providing updates and support while managing expectations.

The dedication of cold case investigators is further exemplified by their resilience in the face of adversity. These professionals often work on cases that have been cold for years, if not decades, and the path to resolution is rarely straightforward. They must contend with the frustration of dead ends, the disappointment of leads that fail to materialize, and the emotional toll of dealing with tragic circumstances. Despite these challenges, they persist, driven by the knowledge that their efforts could one day bring justice to those who have been denied it for so long.

Collaboration is a crucial aspect of cold case investigations. Investigators frequently work alongside forensic experts, psychologists, and other specialists to build a comprehensive understanding of the case. This interdisciplinary approach allows them to draw on a wide range of expertise and perspectives, enhancing their ability to solve complex cases. It also fosters a sense of camaraderie and shared purpose, as professionals from different fields come together in pursuit of a common goal.

Technological advancements have also played a significant role in the dedication of cold case investigators. The development of sophisticated forensic techniques, such as DNA profiling and digital forensics, has opened new avenues for solving cases that were previously deemed unsolvable. Investigators must stay abreast of these advancements, continually updating their skills and knowledge to remain effective in their work. Their dedication to professional development is a testament to their commitment to justice, as they harness the power of technology to uncover the truth.

The impact of cold case investigations extends beyond the resolution of individual cases. By bringing perpetrators to justice, investigators contribute to the prevention of future crimes, as offenders are held accountable for their actions. Their work also serves as a deterrent to potential criminals, reinforcing the message that justice will be pursued, regardless of how much time has passed. This dedication to upholding the law and protecting communities is a driving force behind the tireless efforts of cold case investigators.

For those considering a career in this challenging yet rewarding field, it is essential to understand the qualities that define a successful cold case investigator. Patience, persistence, and a strong sense of justice are paramount, as is the ability to work collaboratively and communicate effectively. Prospective investigators should also be prepared for the emotional demands of the job, developing strategies for managing stress and maintaining resilience in the face of adversity.

Training and education play a vital role in preparing individuals for the rigors of cold case investigations. Aspiring investigators should seek out programs that offer a comprehensive understanding of forensic science, criminal psychology, and investigative techniques. Practical experience is also invaluable, providing opportunities to apply theoretical knowledge in real-world scenarios and develop the skills necessary for success in the field.

Ultimately, the dedication of cold case investigators is a testament to the power of perseverance and the enduring pursuit of justice. Their work brings closure to families, restores public confidence in the justice system, and ensures that no case is ever truly forgotten. Through their tireless efforts, they honor the memory of victims and reaffirm the principle that justice delayed is not justice denied.

In reflecting on the dedication of these professionals, we are reminded of the profound impact that one individual, driven by a commitment to truth and justice, can have on the lives of others. Their stories inspire us to support and appreciate the work of cold case investigators, recognizing the invaluable contributions they make to our communities and the broader pursuit of justice.

The Role of Victim Advocacy and Support Groups

Victim advocacy and support groups play a pivotal role in the journey of healing and justice for those affected by crime. Their presence is crucial, providing a lifeline to individuals and families during their most vulnerable moments. Understanding the scope and impact of these groups is essential for anyone navigating the aftermath of a crime, whether as a victim, a supporter, or a professional in the field. By examining their functions and exploring practical ways to engage with these resources, we can better appreciate the profound difference they make in the lives of countless individuals.

At the heart of victim advocacy is the commitment to empower those who have experienced trauma. Advocates often serve as intermediaries between victims and the various entities involved in the criminal justice system. Their primary goal is to ensure that victims' rights are upheld and that their voices are heard throughout the legal process. This involves educating victims about their rights, assisting them in filing necessary paperwork, and accompanying them to court proceedings. Advocates provide clarity and guidance in navigating the often complex and intimidating world of legal procedures, ensuring that victims are fully informed and supported at every step.

Beyond legal assistance, victim advocates offer emotional support and crisis intervention. They understand that the aftermath of a crime can be overwhelming, and their presence provides comfort and stability. Through active listening and empathetic communication, advocates help victims process their emotions and begin the journey toward healing. This compassionate support is invaluable, as it helps victims regain a sense of control and agency, enabling them to make informed decisions about their future.

Support groups complement the work of victim advocates by fostering community and connection among those who have experienced similar traumas. These groups provide a safe and confidential space for individuals to share their stories, express their feelings, and receive validation from others who understand their experiences. The sense of camaraderie that develops within support groups can be a powerful source of healing, as participants draw strength from one another and realize they are not alone in their struggles.

Support groups also serve as a platform for education and skill-building. Facilitators often introduce topics related to coping strategies, self-care, and resilience, equipping participants with practical tools to navigate the challenges they face. By engaging in group discussions and activities, individuals can develop new perspectives and approaches to their situations, empowering them to move forward with confidence.

For those who are new to victim advocacy and support groups, understanding how to access these resources is crucial. Many organizations offer hotlines and online platforms where individuals can connect with advocates and learn about available services. Community centers, hospitals, and law enforcement agencies are also valuable sources of information, often partnering with advocacy groups to provide comprehensive support. Reaching out to these organizations is a critical first step for victims seeking assistance and guidance.

In addition to direct support, advocacy groups often engage in broader efforts to raise awareness and effect change. They may organize public campaigns, workshops, and events to educate the community about issues related to victimization and prevention. By advocating for policy changes and reforms, these groups work to improve the systemic response to crime and enhance protections for victims. Their efforts contribute to a more informed and compassionate society, where the needs of victims are recognized and addressed.

For those considering a career in victim advocacy, it's important to cultivate a range of skills and qualities that will enable them to effectively support individuals in crisis. Empathy and active listening are fundamental, as they foster trust and understanding in interactions with victims. Strong communication skills are also essential, as advocates must convey complex information clearly and effectively. Additionally, resilience and self-care are vital for advocates, who must balance the emotional demands of their work with their own well-being.

Training and education are critical components of preparing for a role in victim advocacy. Many advocates pursue degrees in social work, psychology, or criminal justice, gaining a solid foundation in the principles and practices that underpin their work. Professional development opportunities, such as workshops and certifications, can further enhance advocates' skills and knowledge, ensuring they remain effective and informed in their roles.

The impact of victim advocacy and support groups extends far beyond individual cases. By empowering victims and fostering healing, these groups contribute to the overall well-being and resilience of communities. They remind us of the importance of compassion and solidarity, and the power of collective action to create positive change. Through their tireless efforts, advocates and support group facilitators help build a world where victims are not defined by their experiences, but are supported in their journey toward recovery and empowerment.

For victims, engaging with advocacy and support groups can be a transformative experience, offering hope and healing in the aftermath of trauma. By reaching out and connecting with these resources, individuals can find the support they need to navigate the challenges they face and reclaim their lives. Whether through one-on-one advocacy, group participation, or community involvement, the journey toward healing is one that no victim should have to undertake alone.

In recognizing the invaluable role of victim advocacy and support groups, we are reminded of the profound impact that empathy, understanding, and action can have on the lives of those affected by crime. By supporting and expanding these resources, we can ensure that all victims have access to the assistance and empowerment they deserve, fostering a more just and compassionate society for all.

Coping with Uncertainty and Unanswered Questions

The human mind craves certainty. It seeks patterns, answers, and resolutions to make sense of the world. Yet, life often presents us with situations shrouded in ambiguity, leaving us with uncertainty and unanswered questions. This is especially true for those who endure the agony of unresolved personal or external crises. When faced with such challenges, it becomes essential to develop strategies for coping, allowing individuals to find peace and resilience amidst the unknown.

Consider the story of Emma, who found herself in the throes of uncertainty when her partner vanished without a trace. With each passing day, she oscillated between hope and despair, grappling with questions that had no answers. What happened? Where could they be? The lack of closure was a constant companion, haunting her every thought. Yet, over time, Emma discovered ways to navigate the emotional turbulence and find a semblance of peace.

One of her first steps was to acknowledge her feelings. Suppressing emotions can lead to greater distress, so Emma allowed herself to feel the full spectrum of her emotions— anger, sadness, confusion, and even moments of acceptance.

Journaling became a vital tool for her, providing an outlet for expression and helping her process the whirlwind inside. By putting pen to paper, Emma found clarity and release, enabling her to articulate fears that seemed insurmountable when trapped in her mind.

Emma also realized the importance of setting boundaries with the information she consumed. In an age where news and speculation are ever-present, it was tempting for her to immerse herself in every detail, hoping for a clue or resolution. However, this constant influx of information often heightened her anxiety. By consciously choosing when and how to engage with updates, Emma was able to protect her mental well-being, ensuring that her life wasn't entirely consumed by the uncertainty.

Another crucial aspect of coping with uncertainty is cultivating mindfulness and staying present. Emma found solace in practices that anchored her to the moment, such as meditation and deep-breathing exercises. These practices helped her focus on the here and now, rather than being overwhelmed by an uncertain future or an unchangeable past. By centering herself, she was able to reduce anxiety and find moments of calm amidst the chaos.

Support networks also played an integral role in Emma's journey. Friends, family, and support groups provided a safe space for her to share her experiences and emotions. Surrounding herself with empathetic and understanding individuals reminded her that she was not alone in her struggle. The collective strength and wisdom of her support network offered perspectives and insights that she might not have discovered on her own.

Emma's story also highlights the power of acceptance, not as a surrender to circumstances but as a recognition of what is beyond one's control. Acceptance allowed her to release the constant need for answers and find peace in the unresolved. By acknowledging the limits of her influence, Emma was able to focus on what she could control—her responses, her actions, and her outlook. This shift in perspective was liberating, empowering her to reclaim agency in her life.

For those grappling with uncertainty, it is essential to establish routines and set achievable goals. Structure provides a sense of normalcy and stability, offering a counterbalance to the unpredictability of life. By setting small, attainable goals, individuals can experience a sense of accomplishment, reinforcing a positive mindset and fostering resilience. Emma found that even simple tasks, like taking a walk or preparing a meal, became acts of empowerment, grounding her in the present and reminding her of her capacity to create change.

In moments of uncertainty, it's easy to become consumed by the need for closure, but finding purpose can be a powerful antidote. Emma chose to channel her energy into advocacy, raising awareness for missing persons and supporting others who faced similar situations. This newfound purpose provided meaning and direction, transforming her personal struggle into a force for positive change. By focusing on a cause greater than herself, Emma was able to transcend her own pain and contribute to the broader community.

Coping with uncertainty also requires self-compassion. Emma learned to be gentle with herself, recognizing that her journey was not linear and that it was okay to have setbacks. By practicing self-compassion, she fostered resilience and resilience, allowing her to navigate the challenges with grace and patience. This kindness to oneself is vital, as it creates a nurturing environment for healing and growth.

Ultimately, Emma's story serves as a testament to the human capacity for resilience in the face of uncertainty. Her journey underscores that while we may not always have answers, we can choose how we respond to the unknown. By embracing our emotions, seeking support, and finding purpose, we can navigate the complexities of life with strength and grace.

For anyone facing uncertainty, remember that it is a shared human experience. While the circumstances may differ, the emotions and challenges are universal. By drawing on the collective wisdom of those who have walked similar paths, we can find guidance and inspiration to light our way. Each step forward, no matter how small, is a victory, a testament to the resilience that resides within us all.

Emma's story is just one of many, but it illustrates the transformative power of coping strategies in the face of the unknown. By cultivating mindfulness, seeking support, and embracing acceptance, individuals can find peace amidst uncertainty and unanswered questions, forging a path toward healing and renewal.